JAMAICAN COCKTAILS & MIXED DRINKS

Selected and Edited by
Mike Henry

LMH Publishing Limited

ACKNOWLEDGEMENTS

In my effort to produce this book and to create and list recipes, I have used many a reference book, chief of which has been Anthony Hogg's *Cocktails and Mixed Drinks* (Hamlyn); *Cocktails and Mixed Drinks* by Eddie Torado (Hamlyn); *Mr. Boston's Drink Guide* and *The Official Mixer's Guide* by Patrick Duffy and Robert Misch.

I would like to pay special thanks to my friend Gregg Lee, whose idea for a Caribbean drink book it was and to the numerous bartenders throughout the Caribbean who generously contributed their recipes.

This new edition was supported by the award-winning Sandals Hotel chain which provided the setting for the photographs and the Sandals gift for concocting romantic and exciting drinks like '*Cool 'N' Nice*', '*Blue Murder*', '*Love Potion*' and '*Virgin's Kiss*', which are all captured on pages of this book.

Mike Henry
Publisher

(On holidays *at Sandals*, measurements for cocktails are at bar tenders' discretion)

To Stella,
Andrew, Mark, Denise, Nicholas and Gregg whose idea it was.

Le Meridien Jamaica Pegasus Hotel
Dr. Ian Sangster & Co. Ltd./Lascelles Wines & Spirits
Ole Nassau Liqueurs
Angostura
Sandals

Photograph on Cover: Ray Chen

Published by LMH Publishing Ltd.
7 Norman Road, Kingston, Jamaica
Copyright 1980 Mike Henry & T.E.P. Bahamas Ltd.
First Edition 1980
Second Edition 1996
Revised Edition 2001

ISBN 976-8184-12-4

Printed in Jamaica by: Smith's Printing Services Ltd. 5 Content Avenue, Kingston 11.

CONTENTS

INTRODUCTION

Since the early 1950s, I could be what is called a globetrotter and have, therefore, in my time become the imbiber and not the dispenser. However, whether it has been in the pubs or the hotels cocktail lounges or the rum bars of the Caribbean, I have always admired those dispensers of alcoholic dreams.

Since then there have not been many changes to the indigenous world of Caribbean cocktails. We have seen however the growth of the visitor market and by extension the exposure of greater numbers of the world's population to the products of the Caribbean.

Within the visitor industry we have also seen the rise of the all inclusive resorts through the innovative spirit of its pioneer John Issa and Super Clubs Group and subsequently Butch Stewart of the Sandals Group.

In the Bahamas the advent of the Atlantis development on Paradise Island speaks of the growth of the Caribbean marketplace.

So here's to good drinking while you calmly or excitedly cavort across the expanse of the Blue Caribbean.

STOCK FOR A BASIC BAR

The basic Caribbean bar should include white and dark rums, rum punch and 151% rum, Ole Nassau flavoured rum liqueurs of coconut, pineapple and banana, Caribbean liqueurs such as Curacao, pimento liqueur and Sangster's special liqueurs of ginger, wild orange, ortanique and spirit of Forget-me-not, Campari and Angostura bitters.

To complete the bar one must include scotch and rye whisky and bourbon, brandy, gin, vodka, vermouth (both sweet and dry), plus other basic liqueurs such as Advokaat, cherry brandy, Creme de Cacao, Creme de Menthe (both green and white) Cointreau, Drambuie, soft drinks and juices should include papaya and mango juice, pineapple juice, bitter lemon, cola, Jamaican dry ginger ale, soda water, tonic water, orange juice, lemon juice, lime juice and tomato juice.

BASIC BAR EQUIPMENT

Cocktail Shaker or blender
Mixing glass and spoon
Measures — ½ and 1 oz.
Ice bucket and tongs
Corkscrew
Strainer
Openers (bottle and can)
Swizzle sticks
Coasters
Napkins
Cloth for glasses
Nutmeg
Grater
Oranges
Lemons
Cherries (maraschino)
Olives
Cocktail onions
Straws
Limes
Onions
Mint
Cucumber
Cloves
Cinnamon
Sugar
Salt
Cayenne

TIPS FOR MAKING GOOD DRINKS

- Always measure your ingredients. Don't guess!

- Stir all clear drinks. e.g. Martinis with ice.

- Blend in electric blender or shake well all drinks which contain fruit juices or cream. e.g. Whisky Sour or Brandy Alexander, to acquire a perfect blend.

- If possible serve all drinks in chilled glasses. Glasses may be chilled by placing them in the freezing compartment of your refrigerator for a few minutes or by placing a few cubes of ice in them prior to mixing the drink. Discard this ice before serving.

- Serve drinks ice cold. Have plenty of clean ice on hand. Put ice in glass, shaker or mixer first to chill quickly.

- Use fresh juices whenever possible.

- Use only the 'zest', the green part of the lemon/lime/orange when peel is requested. Do not include the 'pith' which is the white, bitter membrane of the rind.

- Always try to present a cocktail as attractively as possible.

- Drink the cocktail as soon as possible after mixing.

- Use clean, unchipped glasses.

- Add peel or cherry *after* the drink has been shaken or mixed.

- As a rule, *shake* hard to blend ingredients like fruit juices. *Stir* drinks made with clear liquors. For a 'frothy collar' on drinks, add a tablespoon of egg-white before shaking.

- In simple drinks, ice comes first then liquor, then mix. If a recipe uses sugar, it comes first. If soda is used it should be *cold* and added last. Always use freshly made ice for each round of drinks. Pre-chill glasses by filling with cracked ice. Store wet glasses in freezer to frost.

- Carbonated beverages should be the last ingredient added to a drink.

MEASUREMENTS

In Britain the smallest practical unit of liquid capacity is the fluid ounce (fl. oz.), in America it is a liquid ounce, and in the Western Europe the centilitre (cl.).

Dessertspoon	=	¼ fl. oz.
6 out measure	=	5/6 fl. oz.
5 out measure	=	1 fl. oz.
4 out measure	=	1¼ fl. oz.
Pony (USA)	=	1 fl. oz (approx.)
Jigger (USA)	=	1½ fl. oz (approx.)

Cocktail glasses vary from 2/3½ oz. 2½ is an average UK size
4 oz. wine glasses (USA) is a good size for sours, like vodka and tomato juice.
A UK size is a 5 oz. wine glass.

14 cl	=	5 fl oz = 1 gill or noggin
23 cl	=	UK 8 oz wine glass
28.4 cl	=	10 fl oz. = UK ½ pt.
33 cl	=	12 oz. wine glass
55 cl	=	UK pint
75 cl	=	One reputed qt. = usual wine bottle
100 cl	=	1 litre
1.14 litre	=	40 fl. oz. = 80 gills = 1 Imperial Qt. = ¼ Imp. Gallon.

Some Standard Bar Measures:

1 dash	=	1/6 teaspoon (1/32 ounce)
1 teaspoon	=	1/8 ounce
1 tablespoon	=	3/8 ounce
1 Pony	=	1 fl. oz.
1 wine glass	=	4 ounces
1 split	=	6 ounces
1 cup	=	8 ounces

Alcoholic Contents in terms of Proof Spirit:

		Vol. % Alcohol added
Beer	8.5%	4.8
Gin	67%	38.19
Liqueurs	52.7%	30.03
Rum	60%	39.33
Whisky	70%	39.90
Wine	18.35%	10.46

CONVERSION TABLE

To change from	To	Multiply by
grams	ounces	0:035
ounces	grams	28.35
kilograms	pounds	2.205
pounds	kilograms	0.454
centilitres	fluid ounces (U.K.)	0.352
centilitres	liquid ounces (U.S.A.)	0.338
gallons (U.K.)	litres	4.50
gallons (U.S.A.)	litres	3.80
litres	centilitres	10.00

Temperature:

°F to °C deduct 31 and multiply by 5/9.
°C to °F multiply by 9/5 and add 32.

ABOUT OUR CARIBBEAN PRODUCTS

Rum

Rum was the drink of the slaves on the plantations of the British West Indies. On the British side of the world rum was not known until Admirals Penn and Venables captured Jamaica in 1655, but it was known to the Europeans from when Columbus discovered the island in 1494, and he, it was who actually brought cane cuttings to the W.I. from the Canaries. Rum had been known to China, Cyprus, Sicily in Roman times, but climate was to make the West Indies the 'greatest producer.'

Rum is a spirit distilled direct from the sugar cane and aged in oak casks and it is perhaps, one of the 'hottest' of spirits. The traditional dark, pungent, heavy bodied rums of Jamaica fall definitely into this hot category, while the odourless and almost colourless come chiefly from Puerto Rico and Cuba. In Jamaica the two most famous brands are Sangsters and Appleton; in Puerto Rico 'Ron Rico' and Bacardi; in Guyana 'Demerara' and 'Santigo'; in Barbados 'Mount Gay'; in Trinidad 'Old Oak'.

The making of rum consists of the freshly cut sugar cane being crushed in rollers. The juice is then clarified in large tanks to concentrate the sugar and leave a thick syrup after surplus water is drawn off. This liquid is then crystallised leaving a sugary molasses which is useless until distilled. This is then taken to the distillery where water and yeast is added to the molasses and allowed to ferment. The selection of yeast and the fermentation time governs the final character of the rum. Generally sugar caramel provides the colouring with a minimum aging period of 3 years.

Rum is accepted as superior to Vodka, Whisky and Gin in the sense that sugar being already present in the cane, there is no need for a preliminary malting process necessary to convert starch to sugar. Thus rum retains much more flavour.

For cocktails a light bodied and white rum is best. Jamaican rum is certainly the best for hot drinks. Rum itself blends nicely with fruit juices and most liqueurs.

Light rums are dry and available in two varieties - light and dark. These can be had from Jamaica, Puerto Rico, Cuba, Virgin Islands and to the lesser degree Dominican Republic, Haiti, Mexico, Hawaii and the Philippines.

Rum ...

The heavier bodied rums are darker and sweeter and through a slower fermentation process they are fuller and richer. Rums in this category are usually from Jamaica, Guyana, Martinique, Trinidad and Barbados.

The Story of Rum

FERMENTATION

Fermentation is the process whereby sugar is converted into Alcohol and Carbon Dioxide by the action of yeast. The main ingredient in the manufacture of Rum is molasses which is a by-product of the production of cane sugar. The molasses, containing about 60% sugar is mixed with water to bring the sugar content down to about 15%. The mixture is then pasteurized and pumped into the fermenting tanks. The fermentation of the sugar starts when a test tube of yeast is cultured in a sterile solution of molasses and water. Yeast is constantly multiplying so the culture is successively transferred to larger quantities of molasses and water (the mixture being called "live wash"), until it reaches the 2000 gallon "Bubb Tun" stage. By this time there are enough yeast cells to tackle the 24,000 gallons of live wash that has been pumped into one of the fermenters. There are approximately 26,000 lbs. of dissolved sugar in one of these fermenters and the original yeast culture, now many times multiplied is able to convert all this sugar into 3,000 gallons of rum and 13,000 lbs. CO_2 within a mere 30 hours. The bubbles and motion appearing on the surface of the fermenter are due entirely to the rapid movement of yeast and the CO_2 given off from its cells. When the sugar is used up the yeast dies from lack of nutrient and the mixture known as "dead wash" is now ready for distillation. About four 24,000 gallon fermenters are distilled each day so the mixing and fermentation pro-

14

cess goes on 24 hours a day with a clock-like regularity. It is interesting to note that the wash is distilled about 5 days after the original test tube of yeast was cultured and at the end of the final phase there are about 150 lbs. of dead yeast cells left at the bottom of the fermenter. It takes about 1½ gallons of molasses to produce 1 gallon of rum.

DISTILLATION

Rum is one of the purest alcoholic beverages because the fermentation takes place with sugar as the raw material whereas with some spirits the starch in the grain first has to be converted to sugar before the fermentating process can begin. Distillation is the process whereby the alcohol in the dead wash is separated from the water (originally used to dilute the molasses) since alcohol boils at a lower temperature than water. The two methods of distilling used are the pot still and continuous still.

The Pot Still — is basically a kettle which is used to contain the dead wash. Steam is applied to the kettle and the vapour given off is condensed and collected in three separate containers. The three products recovered are rum, (with an 85% alcohol content) high wine and low wine. The rum is put into storage tanks and the wines which have lower concentrations of alcohol are redistilled in the next cycle of the pot still.

The Continuous Still — consists of three gigantic columns, each having a source of steam at their base. The first column is used for stripping the weak solution of alcohol from the wash and the other two are used to purify and concentrate the alcoholic vapours. The columns consist of trays with perforations and downpipes that allow the liquid to flow from one tray to the next going down the column. The steam rises through the perforations and drives the alcohol vapours up the columns.

These vapours condense on the top trays and the liquid is drawn off the trays and cooled before going to the product tanks. The quality of the product depends on how high up the column the condensate is drawn off.

Thus, a mild rum product as well as the purest alcohol can be made on this still. The alcohol made is used in the manufacture of gin, vodka and liqueurs while the mild rum which is light and dry is aged for future consumption.

MATURATION AND BLENDING

Rum when new can be harsh to the taste so it must be aged for many years in 40 gallon oak casks. Oak is permeable so the rum breathes and air passing through the pores of the wood mellows the rum and alters the taste. At the same time the rum takes on some

colour from the oak. On going through a warehouse one will notice the pleasant smell and temperature in the building. This is caused by evaporation of the rum vapour through the pores of the wood which in itself has a cooling effect. There are losses during the process of aging but nothing has ever been found to replace this system of producing a mellow, smooth product.

Once the rum has been aged the contents of each cask are carefully tested by experienced blenders and then mixed in 10,000 gallon oak vats where the process of "marrying the blends" takes place. Brands of rum are derived from varying mixtures of pot still and continuous still products, the former gives the rum its character and the latter the lightness. A dark rum is made by the addition of caramel and the white rums are made by passing the blend through activated charcoal.

The blended rums are then reduced in strength by the addition of purified water and after filtering and polishing they are bottled in the most modern filling machines.

WHITE RUM:
Light, smooth and mellow and one of the best rums. The favourite drink of millions around the world is white rum - in all its forms - and no other white rum can claim to be more mixable or more versatile than Jamaican White. Because of its unique blend, it maintains its subtle taste and delicate aroma in all drinks in which it is served.

APPLETON SPECIAL:
The pride of Jamaica and found in over 800 cities and towns throughout the world. Made from a superb blend of fine old Jamaican Rums, Appleton Special has a taste and a smoothness all its own.

18

RUMS OF THE ISLANDS

THE BAHAMAS — These 700 islands although not their own sugar producers, have in their very special way taken the best rums of the Caribbean and by a very special blending process produced rum liqueurs of unmatched quality. The Bahamas Blenders, producers of these fine liqueurs is located on the island of New Providence in the country's capital of Nassau after which the liqueurs are named.

BARBADOS — The island with its high literacy rate and very British traditions, produces a lighter bodied rum tending to medium and many of its fine aged rums can almost be drunk as a liqueur. Sugar cane is the island's main crop and due to the lack of fresh water supplies most of the cane fields have to be irrigated; most of the island's rums are made from molasses in pot or continuous stills. The chief brand being 'Mount Gay'.

CUBA — Cuba, once the home of Ron Bacardi, is the largest of the Caribbean islands and was once the major supplier of light rums. However, under the Castro government, exports ended and most of the major distillers moved to other parts of the Caribbean. Distillation in continuous stills from a molasses base produces a very light rum with a fragrant refreshing taste. The two main rums are 'Carta Blanca' and 'Carta Oro' a golden rum coloured with caramel).

CURACAO — This fine island of Dutch colonial history is the home of that famous liqueur of the same name, 'Curacao' liqueur.

FRENCH GUYANA — This country produces two types of white rums at two distilleries — Mirande and Prevot but these are almost totally for local consumption.

GUADELOUPE—This island is one of the two major suppliers of French rums of the full-bodied pot-still type. Most of its production is shipped in bulk to France for further maturation and bottling. Some of the local distilleries producing rum are Fort Ille, Tabanon, Longueteau, Routa, Bourdon, Bologne Lassere, Neron and Peres Blancs.

GUYANA — Although part of the Latin American mainland due to its former British colonial status, its rums are classified as Caribbean. The most famous of its rums is 'Demerara', named after the river which irrigates most of the sugar cane fields. Like the sugar which bears its name, its is dark and rich. 'Demerara' rum which is made from the molasses left after the production of sugar is fermented very rapidly (48 hours the maximum) this gives a lightness of the spirit. The rapid

19

fermentation also gives the rum less depth; further distillation in pot or continuous stills take the spirit to a high strength. Close to Georgetown are distillers such as Enmore, Diamond, Versailles and Uitvlugt.

HAITI – This, the first independent negro nation produces most of its cane in the shelter of high mountains on the northern hook of the island. The cane juice is distilled without being allowed to ferment and using the double pot still distillation (the cognac process) gives the medium to full bodied rums a considerable fragrance and medium alcoholic strength.

The first distillation gives a clear rum known locally as 'Clairin'. This is used locally as a cheap drink and has an important part in voodoo rites as the libation offered to the spirit gods. The second distillation gives the true Haitian rum – a medium, very full-flavoured, aromatic spirit. Some of the main distilleries are Damien of Rum Barbancourt (considered to be one of the finest Caribbean rums), Rhum Nazon, Rhum Tesserot and Rhum Champion.

JAMAICA – Often described as the Bordeaux of the Caribbean, the traditional Jamaican rums are full flavoured, dark with a rich aroma. These were the rums supplied to the British navy for some 200 years and were commonly called "Wedderburn' and 'Plummer').

Today, Jamaica under the Appleton brand produces the full range of rums from molasses with distillation taking place in three main ways and producing three distinctive rums.

The light flavoured rums are produced in continuous stills after a short fermentation. Medium bodied pot still rums are made from cane juice mixed with molasses to give a fine aroma.

Heavy, slow fermented pot still rums of the Wedderburn and Plummer types have a dark, rich fragrance.

The local rum drink is 'Whites' – a strong clean white rum consumed either straight or with any chaser from water through milk to coke. In its first distillation it is known as 'culu culu' and this is often times used locally to make rum punch of the strongest types.

MARTINIQUE – Home of the major French-based rums. Most of the rums are made from cane juice and are sold either without casking as 'Grappe Blanche' or are matured to take on the wood colour. Grappe Blanche is the main ingredient of Martinique's rum punch, a popular island drink. White rum is also made from cane juice at such distilleries as Duquesne and Clement. The main brands being 'Genippa', Grand Case', 'Vald'or' (a ten year old rum), 'Rhum Clement', 'Rhum St. James' of the Martinique rums. Others such as 'St. James' and 'Vive' (made only from molasses) are similar to the heavy Jamaican flavour and aroma.

PUERTO RICO – This island has taken over from Cuba as the leading producer of White rums. Home of the Bacardi rums, Puerto Rican rums are traditionally distilled from molasses in a continuous still to a high strength but retaining a lightness and good aroma. As most are intended to be clear, Puerto Rican rums are very seldom stored in barrels. Known brands in addition to Bacardi, are 'Ron Rico', 'Ron Viejo', 'Maraca', 'Vanioca,' 'Don Q' and 'Merito'.

TRINIDAD — This oil producing, carnival country produces good quality medium bodied rums from quick fermented molasses distilled in continuous stills with a high alcoholic content. The most famous brand is 'Old Oak'.

VIRGIN ISLANDS — These three islands St. Thomas, St. John's and St. Croix made rums similar to Trinidad's and is sold under the brand name 'Cruzan'.

LIQUEURS

Sangster's Old Jamaica Liqueurs

High in the Blue Mountains of Jamaica are created some of the finest liqueurs in the world. These liqueurs are blended from selected aged Jamaican rums and a range of exotic fruits and spices. The warm spirited heart of these liqueurs is — a balanced blend of carefully selected aged Jamaican rums.

Lovingly created in the cool tropical climate, these liqueurs have gained gold medals at international wine and spirits contests in London (1976) and Bristol (1978) and are superb after-dinner drinks or provide the basis of a number of intriguing mixed drinks. Sangster's Jamaican Coffee Liqueur is the finest of Caribbean Coffee Liqueurs.

Flavours created are:

- Wild Orange — a blend of spirits and orange flavour.
- Blue Mountain Liqueurs — a blend of rum and Blue Mountain Coffee.
- Liqueur Ortanique — a blend of rum and ortanique.
- Pimento Dram
- The Jamaican Creams — using both rich, full European dairy cream and our own local rum, fruits and spices.

Ole Nassau Rum Liqueurs

These fine Rum Liqueurs are produced from the finest rums and flavourings to commemorate the 250th Anniversary of Parliament in the Bahamas.

These liqueurs are lovingly blended and crafted in three very tropical flavours:

● Coconut Rum   ● Pineapple Rum   ● Banana Rum

Sangster's Coffee Rum Liqueur

This world-renowned liqueur with Jamaican Rum base is one of the rewarding things about a visit to the Caribbean. Try it with a measure of cognac and champagne and garnish with a black cherry.

Tia Maria

This famous Coffee Liqueur is made from sugar cane and coffee. One favourite way to serve it is with milk over ice and a dash of nutmeg.

OTHERS

Angostura 78°

It is the best known brand of bitter (Q.V.), a few drops being used to flavour aperitif and longer drinks. Originally the invention of the Frenchman Dr. Siegert, in Venezuela circa 1825, to combat disease among Bolivar's troops, it is now compounded in Trinidad. Angostura smooths and blends the taste of cocktails, adding a harmonizing touch to your favourite spirits and light wines to create the perfect cocktail for every mood.

Campari 42°

A bitter-sweet Italian aperitif of spirit and wines, named' after its inventor; drunk with soda, straight or with sweet vermouth (Americano). It is said that the nuts from which this aperitif is made is found only in the Bahamas. Truly a drink for the connosieuer. Try a Bahamian Delight.

Curacao 52.5°

Originally from the Caribbean island of Curacao; a distillation of oranges steeped in Spirit. The blue is the white artifically coloured.

RUM BASED DRINKS

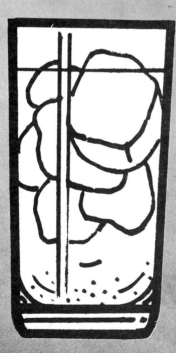

Mac made his way along the office corridor. He looked intently at the letters on the door and with narrowed eyes turned the handle and walked in.
'Ist thish Alcoholicks Anonymush? he lisped.
'Yes, sir! D'you wish to join?'
No, tae resign.'

BIG BAMBOO

2 oz. Jamaican Rum
¼ oz. lime juice
¼ oz. Grenadine

¼ oz. Triple Sec
1 oz. orange juice

Shake, pack a large mug or tall glass with powdered ice and pour mixture over same.
Garnish with a sprig of mint and serve with a straw.

RUM BLOODY MARY

2 ozs. Caribbean White Rum
4¼ ozs. tomato juice
¼ oz. lime juice
Salt

3 or 4 dashes Worcestershire Sauce
3 or 4 drops Tabasco sauce

Stir with cracked ice. Strain and serve.

BUCCANEER PUNCH

3 ozs. Caribbean Special Rum
1 oz. lime juice
3 teaspoons sugar

Dash of Angostura Bitters
1 cup cracked ice

Shake and pour unstrained into glass, adding a slice of lime and a little nutmeg. Serve with a straw.
For tall drinks top up with soda water.

RUM DAIQUIRI

2½ ozs. Sangster's White Rum
¼ oz. lime juice

2 level teaspoons sugar
3 to 4 ice cubes

Shake and strain contents into a cocktail glass.

HIGHWIND

2 ozs. Jamaican Special Rum
1 oz. pineapple juice
½ oz. lime juice

1 oz. Grenadine syrup
½ oz. orange juice

Shake and serve with ice and a slice of orange.

RUM SCREWDRIVER

1½ ozs. Sangster's White Rum
3 ozs. orange juice

A pinch of sugar (optional)
3 or 4 ice cubes

BAHAMA MAMA (Bahamas)

1¼ oz. rum
3 oz. pineapple juice
¼ oz. lemon juice
¼ oz. Angostura Bitters

1 oz. Creme de Cassis
3 oz. orange juice
Dash of Grenadine Syrup
Dash of nutmeg

Shake well and serve in a tall glass.

BANANA DAIQUIRI

1½ ozs. Rum
1 tablespoon Curacao
1½ ozs. lime juice
1 cup crushed ice

1 teaspoon sugar
1 sliced medium-sized banana

Combine ingredients in a blender and blend at low speed for five seconds. Then blend at high speed until firm.
Pour into champagne glass. Top with a cherry.

BLACK ROSE

A jigger of Rum
1 teaspoon sugar
Cold black coffee
Add ice in a tall glass, stir and serve.

CARIBBEAN CHAMPAGNE

½ teaspoon Rum
½ teaspoon Creme de Banana
Chilled Champagne

Pour rum and banana liqueur into champagne glass.
Fill with champagne and stir lightly.
Add a slice of banana.

CARNIVAL JUMP-UP

2 ozs. dark rum
½ oz. Grenadine Syrup
½ oz. fresh lime juice

1 oz. fresh coconut cream
Slice of pineapple
Slice of lime

Shake all liquids and pour into a small Bengali glass.
Garnish with pineapple and lime. Serves 6.

CHINESE COCKTAIL

1¹/2 ozs. Rum
1 tablespoon Grenadine
1 dash bitters

1 teaspoon Maraschino
1 teaspoon Triple Sec

Shake with ice and strain into cocktail glass.

CLARENDON COCKTAIL

1½ ozs. Rum
Juice 1 lime
3 teaspoons powdered sugar

1 oz. grapefruit juice
1 dash bitters

Shake with ice and strain into cocktail glass.

COCONUT OAK

1¼ ozs. dark rum
½ oz. gin
½ oz. Carypton
½ oz. fresh lime juice

2 oz. coconut water/milk
½ oz. syrup
2 dashes Angostura bitters
½ coconut shell

Shake all ingredients with crushed ice.
Serve in a coconut shell with straws.
Serves 6.

CREOLE COCKTAIL

1 oz. amber rum
1 oz. dark rum
½ oz. orange juice
½ oz. syrup
1 cherry
Slice of lime

½ oz. Carypton
2 dashes Grenadine syrup
1 dash fresh coconut cream
Sprig of mint

Shake all liquids with crushed ice, then strain into a tall glass.
Garnish with mint, the slice of lime and cherry.

CUBAN COCKTAIL

2 ozs. Rum
1½ ozs. powdered sugar
Juice ½ lime

Shake with ice and strain into cocktail glass.

(A) *Sandals' Pina Colada*   **(B)** *Virgin's Kiss*

DAIQUIRI BERMUDA

3 parts White Rum
1 part lemon or lime juice
1 teaspoon simple syrup

Thoroughly shake ingredients together. Strain into chilled cocktail glass and serve with straw.

DIP-AN-FALL-BACK

2 ozs. Light Rum
½ teaspoon Curacao
1 teaspoon orange juice

1 teaspoon Lemon Juice
1 teaspoon Raspberry syrup

Shake with ice and strain into cocktail glass. Decorate with small slice of pineapple.

EL PRESIDENTE

1 jigger light rum
1/3 jigger Curacao

1/3 jigger dry vermouth
1 dash Grenadine

Shake well with ice and strain into cocktail glass.

FROZEN DAIQUIRI (Stella's Joy)

Crush two cups ice in a blender. Add four jiggers of Light Rum.

1 tablespoon fresh lime juice
2 tablespoons powdered sugar
Blend in by preference either:
½ a very ripe banana or
1/3 cup canned mango fruit or pineapple chunks

The final consistency should be like snow (whatever the flavour chosen). Serve in a stemmed 4 oz wine glass with a straw and topped with a maraschino cherry.

GOOMBAY SMASH (Bahamas)

1¼ ozs. Dark Rum
¾ oz. Ole Nassau Coconut Rum
3 ozs. pineapple juice

¼ oz. lemon juice
¼ oz. Triple sec
Dash of simple syrup

Shake well and serve in a tall glass — with cracked ice, a cherry and sliced lemon on top of glass.

HAVANA COCKTAIL
¾ oz. Light Rum
1½ ozs. pineapple juice
½ teaspoon lemon juice

Shake with ice and strain into cocktail glass.

HURRICANE
1 oz. Dark Rum
1 tablespoon Passion Fruit Syrup

1 oz. Light Rum
2 teaspoons lime juice

Shake with ice and strain into cocktail glass.

KINGSTON No.1
½ ozs. Rum
¼ Kummel

¼ orange juice
1 dash pimento dram

Shake with ice and strain into glass.

KIN-PUPPA-LICK
1½ ozs. Rum Menthe
1½ ozs. Creme de Menthe (white)

1 dash lemon juice

Shake with ice and strain into cocktail glass.

LIMBO
1½ ozs. Dark Rum
½ teaspoon Creme de Menthe
½ teaspoon Triple Sec Curacao

1 tablespoon lime juice
1 teaspoon powdered sugar

Shake with ice and strain into cocktail glass. Add lime slice.

MAI-TAI
2 ozs. Light Rum
1 oz. Curacao
1 Tablespoon lime juice
½ teaspoon powdered sugar.

1 tablespoon Orgeat or
Almond-flavoured syrup.
1 tablespoon Grenadine

Shake with ice and strain into large old-fashioned glass about 1/3 full with crushed ice.

Decorate with Maraschino cherry speared to wedge of fruit. Preferably fresh pineapple.

For a 'hair raiser', top with a dash of 100% proof rum and for a real Caribbean/Hawaiian effect, float an orchid on each drink. Serve with straws.

(A) *Cool & Nice*   **(B)** *Sandals Iced Tea*

MORNING ROSE

½ jigger light rum
½ jigger Curacao

1/3 jigger Grenadine
1/3 jigger lemon juice

Shake well with ice and strain into cocktail glass.

NAKED LADY

½ light rum
½ sweet vermouth
4 dashes apricot brandy

2 dashes Grenadine
4 dashes lemon juice

Shake well with ice and strain into cocktail glass.

NATIONAL

1 1/3 jiggers light rum
1/3 jigger pineapple juice

1/3 jigger apricot brandy
1 cherry

Shake well with shaved ice and strain into glass.
Serve with pineapple stick or wedge and cherry.

OLYMPIA

1 jigger Dark Rum
2/3 jigger cherry brandy

Juice of ½ lime

Shake well with ice and strain into cocktail glass.

PASSION DAIQUIRI

1½ ozs. Rum
1 tablespoon Passion fruit
juice

1 teaspoon powdered sugar
Juice 1 lime

Shake with ice and strain into cocktail glass.

PILOT HOUSE HOTEL
PLANTERS PUNCH

1¼ ozs. Myers Rum
3 ozs. pineapple juice
3 ozs. orange juice
¼ oz. lemon juice

¼ oz. Grenadine syrup
¼ oz. Angostura Bitters
Dash of nutmeg

Shake well and serve in tall glass.

PINA COLADA

3 ozs. Rum
3 tablespoons coconut milk
3 tablespoons crushed pineapple

Place in blender with two cups of crushed ice and blend at high speed for a short time.
Strain into collins glass and serve with straw.

PINEAPPLE COCKTAIL

1½ ozs. Rum
¾ oz. pineapple juice
½ teaspoon lemon juice

Shake with ice and strain into cocktail glass.

PINEAPPLE FIZZ

1 oz. Rum
1 tablespoon lime juice

1 teaspoon Grenadine
1 teaspoon sweet cream

Shake with ice and strain into cocktail glass.
Add a black cherry soaked in rum.

PIRATE'S PUNCH

2 parts Dark Rum
1 sweet vermouth

1 dash Angostura Bitters

Stir well with ice and strain into glass.

PLANTERS COCKTAIL

1½ ozs. Jamaica Rum
½ teaspoon powdered sugar
Juice lemon

Shake with ice and strain into cocktail glass.

PLANTERS PUNCH

3 parts Jamaican rum
1 part lime juice
2 parts sugar syrup
3 parts water including ice or soda
A dash of Curacao or Angostura (optional)

Serve in tall glass with cherries and orange slices. Each Caribbean island makes this drink with its own native rum.

PORT ROYAL

1 pt. Jamaican rum
1 pt Sangster's Coffee Liqueur
1 teaspoon lime juice

Serve over ice, sip and listen for the sunken Port Royal Church bells to ring.

PUERTO RICO MIX

1½ ozs. Light Rum
1 oz. Dark Rum
1 teaspoon Absinthe substitute
¼ teaspoon Grenadine

1 tablespoon lemon juice
1 tablespoon cola drink

Shake with ice and strain into old-fashioned glass over ice cubes.

PUNCH-A-CREME

6 ozs. white rum
3 ozs. dark rum
1 egg

6 ozs. condensed milk
6 ozs. evaporated milk

Whisk all ingredients together. Serve in short glasses over ice cubes. Serves 6.

RUM & COCONUT WATER

1 oz. Rum over ice topped with fresh coconut water.

RUM & COKE (Cuba Libre)

1 oz. Rum over ice topped with Coke
in a highball glass.
Add a squeeze of lime or lemon.

RUM & GINGER ALE

1 oz. rum over ice topped with ginger ale.

RUM & TONIC

1½ ozs. White Rum over ice cubes in a highball glass

Fill with tonic water and add a squeeze of lime or lemon.

RUM & WATER

1½ ozs. Rum over ice cubes in an old-fashioned glass

topped with plain water.

RUM COLLINS

2 ozs. Old Oak Rum   1 teaspoon powdered sugar
Juice 1 lime

Shake with ice and strain into collins glass.
Add several cubes of ice, fill with carbonated water and stir.
Decorate with slice of lemon and a cherry. Serve with a straw.

RUM DAISY

Whereas crustas are served cold, the ice remaining behind in the
shaker, daisies are 'On the Rocks' drinks with raspberry syrup.
Lemon juice and fruit being added to the spirit chosen.

Fill a goblet with ice.   Put in a shaker
1½ oz. rum   ¾ oz. raspberry syrup and
                                 the juice of ½ lemon.

Shake and strain into goblet. Add soda and garnish with fruit.

RUM DUBONNET

1½ ozs. Mount Gay Rum
1½ teaspoons Dubonnet
1 teaspoon lemon juice

Shake with ice and strain into cocktail glass.

RUM FRAPPÉ

Place 1 scoop orange or lemon sherbet in a champagne glass and cover
with rum as desired. Stir and serve.

RUM RICKEY

1½ ozs. Mount Gay Rum
Juice ½ lime
Pour into highball glass over ice cubes and fill with carbonated water
and ice cubes.
Stir and add a wedge of lime.

RUM SOUR

2 ozs. Old Oak Rum
½ teaspoon powdered sugar
Juice ½ lemon

Shake with ice and strain into sour glass.
Decorate with a half slice of lemon and a cherry.

SANTIAGO

2 jiggers Bacardi Rum
2 dashes Grenadine

4 dashes lime juice

Stir well with ice and strain into glass.

SHARK'S TOOTH

1 jigger light rum
½ jigger 151 proof rum
½ jigger lemon juice

½ jigger lime juice
Dash sugar syrup
Dash Grenadine

Pour into large glass with ice. Top with soda.

SORREL APPETIZER

1 lb. prepared sorrel
2 ozs. grated green ginger

6 pts. boiling water

Mix ingredients together, cover and leave overnight. Strain and add rum and sugar to taste. Serve over crushed ice.

SPANISH TOWN

1 jigger medium rum
2 dashes Curacao

Shake with shaved ice and strain into glass. Serve with a grating of nutmeg.

STARAPPLE APPETIZER

6 starapples
2 tablespoons Demerara Rum

2 teaspoons lime juice
Angostura Bitters

Cut starapples in half, remove pulp and mix with rum and sugar and lime juice.
Add a few drops of bitters. Serve chilled in pint glasses.

SUFFERING BASTARD

2 jiggers Demerara Rum
1 jigger light rum
Juice of 1 lime

½ jigger Mai-Tai mix (or
make your own —
½ Curacao, ½ Orgeat)

Garnish with strip of cucumber rind.

SURPRISED

2 jiggers Old Oak Rum
1 jigger Kummel

1 jigger orange juice
1 dash pimento dram

Shake well with shaved ice and strain into glasses.

TRINIDAD

1½ jiggers dark rum
Juice of ½ lime

1 teaspoon powdered sugar
3 dashes Angostura Bitters

Shake well with ice and strain into glass.

TRINIDAD SWIZZLE

1 oz. Old Oak Rum
1 oz. amber rum
1 oz. Grand Marnier
¼ oz. lime juice
2 dashes Grenadine syrup

½ oz. mango juice
Sugar cane stick
Cherry
Sprig-of-mint
Slice of orange

Shake liquids with crushed ice, then pour into a tropical glass.
Add more crushed ice, and garnish with a slice of orange, the cherry
and sugar cane stick.

VIRGIN ISLAND TWIST

1 oz. Mount Gay Rum
1 oz. pineapple juice

¼ teaspoon Grenadine
¼ teaspoon Maraschino

Shake with ice and strain into cocktail glass.

WHITE RUM & SORREL LIQUEUR

To make sorrel, pour boiling water over ½ lb. sorrel flowers from
which the petals have been removed. Cool, strain and sweeten to
taste. Mix this with one pint white rum and let it simmer for a few
days. Add Jamaican ginger to taste and drink as an after dinner
liqueur.

YELLOW BIRD (Bahamas)

1½ ozs. rum
3 ozs. pineapple juice
¼ oz. orange juice
¾ oz. Creme de Banana
Dash of Galliano
¼ oz. Apricot Brandy

Shake well and serve in tall glass.

GIN BASED DRINKS

Then there was Rafferty's attempt to drown his troubles in drink. He found they could swim...

ALLEN SPECIAL

2/3 dry gin
1/3 Maraschino

1 dash lemon juice

Stir well with ice and strain into glass.

ATTA BOY

2/3 dry gin
1/3 dry vermouth

4 dashes Grenadine

Stir well with ice and strain into glass. Serve with a twist of lemon peel.

BARBADOS APRICOT COCKTAIL

1 oz. gin
½ oz. apricot brandy
½ teaspoon Grenadine

2 drops bitters
¼ teaspoon lemon juice
Cracked ice

Shake gin, apricot brandy, Grenadine, bitters and lemon juice with ice. Strain into 2½ oz. cocktail glass and serve.

BERMUDA BRONX

2 measures gin
1 dry vermouth

1 sweet vermouth
Orange juice with ice

Shake well, then strain and serve

BERMUDIANA ROSE

Shake together:

1 pint gin
1 pt. apricot brandy

1 pint Grenadine
1 pint lemon juice

BLUE CURACAO LADY

1 pint gin
1 pint Blue Curacao

1 pint lemon juice
Add a dash of egg white

Shake together and serve.

CREOLE COCKTAIL

1½ ozs. dry gin
1 egg white

1 dash orange bitters
½ teaspoon Grenadine

Shake with ice and strain into cocktail glass.

DEEP SEA

½ Old Tom Gin
½ dry vermouth

1 dash Pernod
1 dash orange bitters

Stir well with ice and strain into glass. Squeeze lemon peel over top and serve with an olive.

GIBSON

Mix a Martini and serve with two pearl onions, in place of lemon peel or olive.

GIMLET

2 measures gin
1 lime juice cordial

Shake well with ice and strain. Add soda water if required.

GIN & IT

Unshaken:

Combine 1 part sweet vermouth in a cocktail glass with 1 part gin. Add a cherry.

GIN & TONIC

Add large measure of gin to tumbler containing ice, fill with chilled tonic water and add a slice of lemon or lime.

GIN TROPICAL

1 oz. gin
1 oz. passion fruit syrup
½ oz. Blue Curacao

Soda water
Maraschino cherry
Slice of orange

Shake gin, syrup and Curacao.
Strain into glass and top with soda water.
Serve with drinking straw, cherry and slice of orange for garnish.

GOLDEN SUN FIZZ

Large measure of gin
Juice of 1 lemon

1 teaspoon sugar
1 egg yolk

Shake well with ice and pour into tumbler containing ice, and fill with soda water.

GRAPEFRUIT COCKTAIL

1 oz. grapefruit juice
1 oz. dry gin
1 teaspoon Maraschino

Shake with ice and strain into cocktail glass. Serve with a cherry.

GUYANESE TWIST

¾ oz. dry gin
¾ oz. Demerara Rum
Juice ¼ lemon

½ teaspoon powdered sugar
¼ teaspoon Grenadine

Shake with ice and pour into cocktail glass.

HAVANA

Shake together 3 parts gin, 3 parts Cointreau and 1 part orange juice.
Serve with ice.

IMPERIAL COCKTAIL

1½ ozs. dry vermouth
1½ ozs. dry gin
1 dash bitters

½ teaspoon Maraschino
(a cherry liqueur)

Stir with ice and strain into cocktail glass.
Serve with a cherry.

JAMAICA GLOW COCKTAIL

1 oz. dry gin
1 tablespoon Claret

1 tablespoon orange juice
1 teaspoon Appleton Rum

Shake and strain (with ice) into cocktail glass.

J.O.S.

1/3 dry gin
1/3 dry vermouth
1/3 sweet vermouth

1 dash brandy
1 dash orange bitters
1 dash lemon or lime juice

Stir well with ice and strain into glass. Twist lemon peel over top.

JOHN COLLINS

Large measure of gin
Juice of 1 lemon

1 teaspoon sugar

Pour into tumbler containing ice cubes and fill up with soda water.
Add a dash of Angostura Bitters, stir and serve with a slice of lemon.

MARTINI

The proportions used in this famous cocktail can be varied to taste, the proportion of gin to dry vermouth should never be less than 4 to 1, but may be as high as 10 to 1.

These ingredients should be put into an ice-cold mixing glass, stirred with ice, and then strained.

An olive or lemon peel can be added according to taste.

MARTINI-DRY

Mix 1 part gin with 1 part dry vermouth and add a dash of orange bitters (optional).

Squeeze zest of lemon peel over the cocktail and optionally add an olive.

MARTINI-MEDIUM

Mix 4 parts gin with 1 part dry vermouth and 1 part sweet vermouth.

MARTINI-SWEET

Mix 2 parts gin with 1 part sweet vermouth and add a cherry.

MAYFAIR

1 measure gin
1 orange juice
3 dashes apricot brandy

Shake with ice and strain.

MOONSHINE

½ dry gin   ¼ Maraschino
¼ dry vermouth   1–2 drops Pernod

Shake well with ice and strain into glass.

NASSAU SHERRY COCKTAIL

1 oz. gin
1 oz. sweet sherry
1 oz. lemon juice

Shake gin, sherry and lemon juice.
Strain into 3 oz. cocktail glass and serve.

NEGRONI
1 measure gin
1 sweet vermouth
1 Campari

Place ingredients into a tall glass with ice.
Add a slice of orange and serve.

OPERA
2/3 dry gin   1/6 Maraschino
1/6 Dubonnet

Stir well with ice and strain into glass. Squeeze orange peel over top.

ORANGE BLOSSOM
1 measure gin
1 juiced orange

Shake well with ice and strain.
A dash of Grenadine can be added to taste.

PAPAYA SLING
1½ ozs. dry gin   Juice 1 lime
1 dash bitters   1 tablespoon papaya syrup

Shake with ice and strain into collins glass over ice cubes. Fill with
carbonated water and stir.

Add a pineapple stick.

PARADISE
1/3 dry gin
1/3 apricot brandy
1/3 orange or lemon juice

Stir well with ice and strain

PERFECT COCKTAIL
1½ ozs. dry gin
¾ oz. dry vermouth
¾ oz. sweet vermouth

Stir gin, dry and sweet vermouth.
Serve in 3 oz. cocktail glass.

PINK GIN

Roll two dashes of Angostura Bitters round a glass, add a large measure of gin and water to taste.

POLO NO.1

1/3 dry gin
1/3 dry vermouth

1/3 sweet vermouth
Juice of 1/3 lime

Shake well with ice and strain into glass.

QUEEN ELIZABETH

½ dry gin
¼ Cointreau

¼ lemon juice
1 dash Pernod

Stir well with ice and strain into glass.

QUEENIE'S COCKTAIL

1 part dry gin
1 part dry vermouth
1 part sweet vermouth

1 part pineapple juice
1 maraschino cherry
1 piece pineapple for decoration

Shake gin, dry and sweet vermouth and pineapple juice.
Serve in cocktail glass with pineapple and cherry.

ROYAL SMILE

½ dry gin
½ Grenadine

2 dashes lemon juice

Stir well with ice and strain into glass.

SATAN'S WHISKERS

1 part gin
1 part Grand Marnier
1 part dry vermouth

1 part sweet vermouth
1 part orange juice

Shake together and add a dash of orange bitters.

SINGAPORE SLING

2 pints gin
1 cherry brandy
Juice of half a lemon

Pour into tumbler containing ice, stir and serve with cold soda water.

SOUTH SIDE

2 jiggers dry gin   ½ tablespoon powdered sugar
Juice of ½ lemon
2 sprigs of fresh mint

Shake well with ice and strain into glass. Add a dash of soda water if desired.

TANGO

2 parts gin   1 part dry vermouth
1 part sweet vermouth   2 dashes Orange Curacao

Shake together and add a dash of orange juice.

TRINITY

1/3 dry gin   1/3 sweet vermouth
1/3 dry vermouth

Stir well with ice and strain into glass.

VIRGIN ISLANDS COCKTAIL

1 oz. dry gin   ¾ oz. Forbidden Fruit
¾ oz. White Creme de Menthe   1 maraschino cherry

Shake gin, Creme de Menthe and Forbidden Fruit.
Strain and serve with cherry in 3 oz. cocktail glass.

WHITE CARGO

½ dry gin
½ vanilla ice cream

No ice is necessary. Shake together till blended and pour into glass.

WHITE WITCH

2 measures gin
1 Cointreau
1 lemon juice

Shake with ice and strain.

YELLOW DAISY

Mix 2 parts gin with 1 part dry vermouth and 1 part Grand Marnier.

VODKA BASED DRINKS

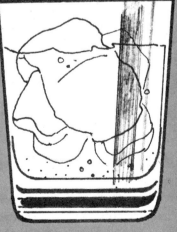

*Prayer of a Catholic girl...
'Oh Virgin Mother, who
didst conceive without
sinning, teach me how to
sin without conceiving.'*

AIR CONDITIONER
2 ozs. vodka
1 oz. Cointreau

Low-calorie coke to taste.
Serve on the rocks.

AQUEDUCT
1½ ozs. vodka
1¾ teaspoons Curacao
1 tablespoon lime juice

1½ teaspoons apricot
brandy

Combine and shake all ingredients and strain into cocktail glass. Add a twist of orange peel.

BAHAMIAN BULLSHOMARY
2 ozs. vodka in tall glass ½ filled with cracked ice
3 ozs. V8 juice
3 ozs. Consomme
Lemon & Worcestershire sauce to suit.
Add a dash of garlic salt and serve before lunch or morning after.

BANANA PUNCH
2 ozs. Smirnoff Vodka
1½ teaspoons apricot brandy
Juice ½ lime

Pour into collins glass filled with crushed ice.
Add tonic water and top with slices of banana and sprigs of mint.

BARBARA (Russian Bear)
1/3 vodka
1/3 Creme de Cacao
1/3 cream

Stir well with ice and strain into glass.

BLACK RUSSIAN
1½ ozs. Smirnoff Vodka
¾ oz. Tia Maria or Sangster's Blue Mountain Coffee Liqueur

Pour over ice cubes in old-fashioned cocktail glass.

BLENHEIM

Shake together 2 parts vodka, 1 part Tia Maria and 1 part fresh orange juice.

BLOODY MARY

2 ozs. vodka
2 drops Tabasco sauce
1 dash Worcestershire sauce
3 cubes ice

¼ oz. lemon juice
tomato juice
Salt and pepper

In 10 oz. glass, put Worcestershire sauce, Tabasco sauce and lemon juice. Add salt and pepper.

Mix together and then add ice cubes and vodka and top with tomato juice.

Serve with swizzle stick.

BULL FROG

1½ ozs. vodka
4 ozs. limeade

Pour vodka into tall glass with ice.
Fill with limeade and stir.

BULL SHOT

Vigorously shake together:

1 oz. vodka
2 ozs. condensed consomme
2 ozs. tomato juice

Add a dash of Worcestershire sauce, tabasco cayenne and celery salt.

EGGHEAD

1½ ozs. vodka
4 ozs. orange juice
Mix and pour into a tall glass with ice.

1 egg in a blender

GODMOTHER

1 jigger of vodka
1 jigger Amaretto di Saronno.
Stir with cracked ice

HARVEY WALLBANGER

1 jigger (1½ ozs.) vodka
3 jiggers orange juice
½ jigger Galliano

Pour vodka in a tall glass filled with ice cubes, pour orange juice and Float Galliano on top.

ICE PICK

1½ ozs. vodka
Lemon-flavoured iced tea

Pour vodka into a tall glass with ice. Top up with iced tea and stir.

JUNGLE JIM

1 oz. vodka
1 oz. Creme de Banana
1 oz. milk

Pour into a short glass with ice and stir.

KANGAROO

1 jigger vodka
½ jigger dry vermouth

Serve with cracked ice and strain into glass. Serve with a twist of lemon peel.

MOSCOW MULE

2 ozs. vodka   Ginger Beer
1 oz. lemon juice   Mint for decoration
3 cubes ice

Put 3 cubes ice in a 10 oz. glass, add vodka and lemon juice and fill with ginger beer.

Decorate with mint and serve.

PINK CRICKETER

3 ozs. vodka   ½ oz. Grenadine
2 ozs. Bourbon   4 ozs. cream
1½ ozs., Ole Nassau Coconut Rum Liqueur

Pour into cocktail shaker with ice.
Shake and strain into cocktail glass.

ROAD RUNNER

1 oz. vodka   ½ oz. Amaretto di Saronno
½ oz. coconut cream

Mix in blender with ½ scoop of crushed ice for 15 seconds.
Rim edge of chilled 4½ oz. champagne glass with a slice of orange.
Dip rim in sugar and nutmeg mixture.
Pour cocktail into prepared glass and top with dash of nutmeg.

RUSSIAN

1 jigger vodka   1 jigger Creme de Cacao
1 jigger dry gin

Stir well with ice and strain into glass.

SALTY DOG

1½ ozs. vodka
5 ozs. grapefruit juice
¼ teaspoon salt.

Pour into highball glass over ice cubes. Stir well.

SCREWDRIVER

1½ ozs. vodka   Slice of orange
3 cubes ice   1 maraschino cherry
Orange juice

Place ice cubes and vodka into a 10 oz. high ball glass and top up
with orange juice.
Garnish with slice of orange and cherry and serve.

SEA URCHIN

1½ ozs. vodka
Grapefruit juice

Serve in a 10 oz. highball glass with ice.
Top up with grapefruit juice.

SUN STROKE

1½ ozs. vodka
3 ozs. grapefruit juice (unsweetened)
Add Triple Sec or Cointreau

Stir together in a short glass filled with ice.

THE MACHETE
1½ ozs. vodka
2/3 glass pineapple juice

Pour into a tall glass with ice. Stir.

VODKA MIST
1½ ozs. vodka   twist of lemon

Pour vodka in a cocktail shaker and add a twist of lemon.
Serve unstrained in old-fashioned glass.

VODKA-ON-THE-ROCKS
1½ ozs. vodka   3 cubes ice

Pour vodka over ice cubes in old-fashioned glass and serve.

VODKA SOUR
2 ozs. vodka   ½ teaspoon powdered sugar
Juice ½ lemon

Shake with ice and strain into sour glass. Decorate with half-slice of
lemon and a cherry.

VODKATINI
2 parts vodka
1 part dry vermouth

Mix ingredients together and add a twist of lemon peel.
A variation of the dry martini, vodka replacing gin.

VOLCANO
2/3 jigger vodka   1 jigger Southern Comfort
1/3 jigger light rum
Shake with cracked ice.

WHITE ELEPHANT
1 oz. vodka   1 oz. milk
1 oz. Creme de Cacao
Pour into a short glass with ice and stir.

YELLOW FEVER
1½ ozs. vodka   4 ozs. lemonade
Add vodka to a tall glass with ice.   Fill with lemonade and stir.

A Tribute to Sandals for the weekend spent drinking and photographing.

Mike Henry
Publisher

From left: Cool "n" Nice, Blue Murder, Blue Monday, Love Potion, Virgin's Kiss and Tequila Sunrise.

In retrospect, it was the kind of weekend that all visitors and those in love would relish.

From the moment we arrived (Dawn & I), until our departure, the Sandals aura cocooned us in warmth and bliss. Indeed, I quickly realized how it was that Butch Stewart was able to hold on to the mantle of "Hotelier of the Millennium".

These four pages of the Sandals bartenders' mixes at its Flagship Hotel, Sandals Montego Bay, appeals to the mood which a Caribbean bar can engender, and why the vacationers at Sandals keep returning year after year, whether it is to Antigua, Jamaica, Turks & Caicos or Bahamas........

'Indeed, There is no place like Sandals'.

Happy drinking and frolicking your cares away.

Blue Monday (PAGE 53)

Vodka
Blue Curaco
7 Up

Lime Juice
Augustan Bitters

Method: Shake

Blue Murder (PAGE 88)

1 oz. Tequila
1 oz. Gold Rum
1 oz. Gin
Dash Lime Juice

1 oz. Vodka
1 oz. Blue Curacao
1 oz. 7 Up

Cool & Nice (PAGE 30)

Cocunut Rum
Apricot Brandy
Pineapple Juice

Orange Juice
Clear Syrup

Love Potion (PAGE 56)

Gold Rum
Triple Sec
Pineapple Juice

Orange Juice
Strawberry Syrup
Lime Juice

Method: Shake

Sandals' Pina Colada

Gold Rum
Coconut Rum
Milk

Pineapple Juice
Clear Syrup
Coconut Cream

Sandals' Iced Tea (PAGE 56)

Rum
Tequilla
Gin

Vodka
Triple Sec
7 Up

Virgins Kiss (PAGE 27)

1 ozs. Gold Rum
1 oz. Blue Curacao
Orange Juice

Pineapple Juice
Clear Syrup
Dash Annisette

Method: Shake

LIQUEUR BASED DRINKS

If one could only teach the English how to talk and the Irish how to listen, life might be civilized...

— Oscar Wilde

BEACHBANGER

2/5 Wild Orange Liqueur
2/5 Old Jamaica Gold Rum
1/5 Lime Juice

Put ice cubes into a cocktail shaker.

Pour the Wild Orange Liqueur, Old Jamaica Gold Rum and lime juice over the ice. Shake well and pour into a highball glass.

Top with soda water or tonic water. Stir gently and serve.

BLUE MOON

1/6 Old Jamaica Gold Rum
2/6 Blue Mountain Coffee Liqueur
3/6 milk

Pour cracked ice into a blender and pour in the ingredients.

Add one medium-sized ripe banana to each pint of milk used.

Blend for two to three minutes until ingredients are smooth and foaming, then pour into cocktail glass.

Add a dash of Sangster's Bitters. Sprinkle lightly with nutmeg or grated coconut and serve.

BLUE RUSSIAN

½ Blue Mountain Coffee Liqueur
½ vodka

Put ice into a chilled old-fashioned glass.

Pour first the vodka and then the Blue Mountain Coffee Liqueur over the ice. Stir and serve.

CIRRHOSIS-ON-THE-SEA

1 measure Sangster's Coffee Liqueur
1 measure Grand Marnier
1 measure Appleton Dark Rum
¾ pt. fresh orange juice
Dash of lime juice

Mix well together in a jug and serve in tall glasses with plenty ice.

COFFEE A LA BLUE MOUNTAIN

1 oz. brandy
½ oz. 151-proof rum
1 oz. Sangster's Coffee Liqueur
½ oz. Curacao
Hot coffee
Whipped cream

Pour the brandy, rum, coffee liqueur and Curacao into a 14 oz. hurricane glass, having first dipped the rum into sugar, if you wish. Fill to within an inch of the top with the rich, full-bodied coffee, and top with a blob of whipped cream.

Blue Monday

COFFEE Á LA MIKE

1½ ozs. Sangster's Coffee Liqueur   Hot coffee
¼ oz. white creme de menthe   Whipped cream

Pour the Sangster's Coffee Liqueur and creme de menthe into an 8 or 10 ozs. pedestal mug, fill to within an inch of the rim with a rich, full-bodied Jamaican Blue Mountain Coffee, and top with a blob of whipped cream.

COFFEE COCONUT

1 oz. Sangster's Blue Mountain   3 cubes ice
    Coffee Liqueur   Nutmeg
2 ozs. brandy   1 coconut

Take top off coconut and remove milk.

Place half the milk and ice cubes into cocktail shaker, then add brandy and Coffee Liqueur. Shake and strain back into the coconut.

Dust with nutmeg – and serve with spoon and drinking straws.

COFFEE EGG NOG

An old-fashioned favourite with a delightful difference.

2 parts Sangster's Coffee Liqueur   1 egg (beaten)
1 part brandy   1 teaspoon sugar
2 parts milk

Beat egg, blend in Coffee Liqueur, milk and sugar, and pour over cracked ice. Sprinkle with nutmeg. As a nightcap, serve warm.

COFFEE 'N COLA

Pour 1½ ozs. Sangster's Coffee Liqueur over ice in a tall glass. Fill with cola and serve.

COFFEE-ON-THE-ROCKS

Pour a generous measure of Sangster's Coffee Liqueur over ice. For a little zip, add a touch of vodka.

COOL MULE

¼ Sangster's Blue Mountain   ¼ Old Jamaican Gold Rum
Coffee Liqueur   ½ Vanilla ice cream

Blend the ingredients until smooth and frothy.
Pour into a tall glass and serve with a cherry.

FORGET-ME-NOT

1/3 Spirit of Forget-Me-Not Liqueur
2/3 Fresh orange juice

Put ice cubes into a cocktail shaker.
Pour the Spirit of Forget-Me-Not Liqueur and chilled fresh orange juice over the ice.
Shake well and pour into a highball glass.
Garnish with a slice of orange and serve.

JAMAICA HOP

1/3 Blue Mountain Coffee   1/3 Light cream
Liqueur   1/3 White cream de cacao
Shake well with ice. Serve in a stemmed glass.

A smooth taste to delight you — on the beach or at the bar.

JAMAICAN COFFEE

1 oz. Sangster's Coffee Liqueur   Hot Coffee
¾ oz. Old Oak Rum

Serve in mug, slightly sweetened.
Top with whipped cream and sprinkle with nutmeg.

MADGE

1 oz. brandy   Hot coffee
1 oz. Sangster's Coffee Liqueur   Whipped cream
1 oz. Creme de Cacao

Pour the brandy, coffee liqueur and creme de cacao into an 8 or 10 oz. pedestal mug, fill to within an inch of the rim with a rich, full bodied Jamaican coffee, and top with a blob of whipped cream.

MEXICAN COFFEE

1 oz. tequila   Whipped cream
1 oz. Sangster's Coffee Liqueur   Powdered cinnamon (optional
Hot coffee   garnish)

Pour the tequila and coffee liqueur into an 8 or 10 oz. pedestal mug, and fill to within an inch of the rim with a rich, full-bodied coffee.
Top with whipped cream, sprinkled with cinnamon if you wish.

ORANGE BAY

Pour 1½ ozs. of Sangster's Wild Orange Liqueur over ice in a highball glass and top up with Jamaican Dry Ginger Ale. Decorate with orange slice and serve.

(A) *Love Potion*   **(B)** *Virgin's Kiss*

ORANGEOTANG

¼ Wild Orange Liqueur
½ Bombay Dry Gin

¼ fresh lemon juice
Sangster's Bitters

Put ice cubes into a cocktail shaker.

Shake a dash of Sangster's Bitters over the ice, then add gin, lemon juice and Wild Orange Liqueur.

Shake until frost forms and pour into a tall glass.

Garnish with a slice of lemon and serve.

PIRATE'S REVENGE

¼ Wild Orange Liqueur
¼ Old Jamaica Rum

½ fresh pineapple juice
Soda water

Put ice cubes into a cocktail shaker.

Pour the Wild Orange Liqueur, Old Jamaica Rum (Gold) and pineapple juice over the ice.

Shake until frothy and pour the mixture into a highball glass.

Top with cold soda water. Stir and serve.

PORT ROYAL GROG

2/5 Wild Orange Liqueur
1/5 brandy
2/5 white wine

2 tablespoons sugar syrup
Clove, cinnamon,
Ground nutmeg

Put Wild Orange Liqueur, brandy and syrup in a warm, punch bowl.

Stir the mixture thoroughly and slowly add the white wine.

Sprinkle the top with cinnamon and nutmeg.

Stir and ladle into punch cups.

SANGSTER'S DELIGHT

1 oz. Blue Mountain Coffee
Liqueur
1 bar spoon simple syrup

1 dash lime juice
1 ripe banana

Blend with crushed ice. Serve in a brandy snifter with a short straw.

An exclusive Caribbean drink that's naturally good tasting.

TROPICAL COFFEE

1 part Sangster's Coffee Liqueur
1 part lime juice

4 parts tonic water

Pour ingredients into a highball glass filled with ice and a slice of lime.

BAHAMAS COW

1 measure Rum Liqueur
2 cups ice cold milk
1 egg

Whisk the egg into the cold milk until it is thoroughly mixed and then pour the creamy mixture into a tall glass with Rum Liqueur.

Stir gently and serve.

BLACK PEARL

1 measure Rum Liqueur   Champagne
1 measure cognac
Chill a champagne glass.

Poor in the Rum Liqueur and cognac and top up to brim with champagne.

Add cracked ice and garnish with a black cherry.

CAFE CALYPSO (Hot)

4 cups freshly percolated coffee   12 tablespoons Rum Liqueur
8 tablespoons Dark Rum   ¼ pt. whipped cream

Blend the Rum Liqueur and rum gently with the coffee in a heat-proof jug. The coffee should be hot but not boiling.

Serve the drink in large coffee cups, sweetening slightly with castor sugar and top with whipped cream.

IRISH COFFEE

2 tablespoons Rum Liqueur   Black coffee
2 teaspoons fine granulated sugar   Whipped cream

Rinse a large wine glass with warm water, and add sugar and fill glass about 2/3 full with hot, strong, black coffee.

Stir. Then add Rum Liqueur and top with a spoonful of softly whipped cream.

JAMAICA COW

1 part Rum Liqueur   4 parts milk

Pour one measure of Rum Liqueur into a highball glass and top up with ice cold milk. Add ice cubes and stir gently.

JAMAICA HOP

1 oz. Rum Liqueur

1 oz. Creme de Cacao

1 oz. Light cream

Shake well with ice and strain into a cocktail glass.

ORANGE DAWN

1 part Rum Liqueur
4 parts fresh orange juice

Serve with plenty ice.

DIANA'S DELIGHT

Coffee ice cream

Vanilla ice cream

Black coffee

Rum Liqueur

Egg whites

Toasted chopped almonds

Pour into a tall parfait glass a layer of chilled black coffee laced with Rum Liqueur.

Add successive layers of vanilla ice cream, whipped egg white sweetened with sugar and finally a scoop of coffee ice cream. Garnish with chopped almonds and pour Rum Liqueur on top.

MORNING MIST

Rum Liqueur on the rocks . . .

With a squeeze of lime . . .

Delightfully different.

PARFAIT A RHUM

1/4 cup Rum Liqueur

1/4 cup strong, clear coffee

1/4 cup evaporated milk, chilled

1/2 teaspoon vanilla

1/4 cup sugar

1 egg

Pinch salt

Cook sugar and coffee together at 230°F, or until syrup spins a thread. Add salt to egg and beat until stiff but not dry. Add Rum Liqueur to syrup. Pour syrup slowly into egg white, beating constantly. Chill and whip milk until very stiff. Fold in egg white and vanilla. Freeze until firm. (Serves 6)

BLACK RUSSIAN
The internationally acclaimed drink of connoisseurs.

1 part Blue Mountain Coffee Liqueur
1 part vodka
2 or 3 ice cubes

Stir well, then sip and enjoy.

BROWN COW
Pour 1 oz. Coffee Liqueur over ice
Fill with fresh milk and serve.

As a special treat, add nutmeg.

KAHLUA 'N SODA
Pour 1½ ozs. Kahlua over ice in a highball glass and add three drops of lemon juice.
Fill with club soda; decorate with lemon slice.
For a little zip, add a touch of vodka.

KAHLUA ORANGE
Pour 1oz. Kahlua over ice and top up with fresh orange juice.
Decorate with orange slice of desired.

TIA ALEXANDRA
1 part Tia Maria
1 part cognac
1 part fresh cream

Shake with cracked ice, strain and serve.

For elegant entertaining, offer your friends a Tia Alexandra, a remarkably smooth and delicious-tasting drink.

T'N'T
A new discovery in delicious refreshment.

Pour 1½ ozs. Tia Maria over ice in a tall glass.

Top up with tonic.
Decorate with lemon slice if desired.

ANTIGUA STINGER

1½ ozs. pimento liqueur
1½ ozs. grapefruit juice
2 ozs. club soda

Serve in a highball glass with ice.

BARBADOS SOUR

¾ oz. pimento liqueur
1½ ozs. cognac
Shake well with cracked ice.

PIMENTO SOUR

1½ ozs. pimento liqueur   ¾ oz. fresh lemon juice
2 ozs. club soda
Serve in a highball glass with ice.

ROSE HALL LIQUEUR

1½ ozs. pimento liqueur   2 ozs. club soda
1½ ozs. orange juice
Serve in a highball glass with ice.

ST.LUCIA JUMP-UP

1½ ozs. pimento liqueur   2 ozs. Club Soda
1½ ozs. pineapple juice

Serve in a highball glass with ice.

WHITE SWAN

1½ ozs pimento liqueur   3 ozs. milk

Put in blender with crushed ice for a few seconds and serve in a champagne glass.

Drinks you can make with OleNassau Banana Rum...

BANANA BLISS

1 part Ole Nassau Banana Rum
1 part brandy

Mix together and serve.

BANANA BOAT

1½ ozs. Banana Rum   Juice ½ lime
1 oz. sweet sherry

Pour ingredients into highball glass over ice cubes and stir. Fill with ginger ale.

BANANA HOP

2 ozs. banana rum   1 teaspoon powdered sugar
6 ozs. milk   1 egg

Shake with ice and strain into collins glass. Sprinkle nutmeg on top.

BANANA MAN

1½ ozs. Banana rum   1 teaspoon powdered sugar
Juice 1 lime   1 tablespoon passion fruit juice

Shake with ice and strain into cocktail glass.

BANANA SONG

½ jigger Banana Rum   2 dashes Grenadine
½ sweet vermouth   4 dashes lemon juice
4 dashes apricot brandy
Shake well with ice and strain.

BANANA TWIST

1/3 Banana Rum   1/3 cream
1/3 Curacao
Shake well with ice and strain into glass.

Drinks you can make with Ole Nassau Coconut Rum...

BAHAMA ROYAL
1 oz. Ole Nassau Coconut Rum
1 oz. Rose Hill 80° Rum
2 ozs. pineapple juice

2 ozs. orange juice
¼ oz. Nassau Royal
2 teaspoons Grenadine

Garnish with sweet cherry.

BAHAMAS SMASH
2 ozs. Ole Nassau Coconut Rum
1 oz. Rose Hill 80° Rum
2 ozs. pineapple juice

1 oz. orange juice
¼ oz Nassau Royal
2 teaspoons Grenadine

Garnish with sweet cherry.

BLENDERS ROCK
1 oz. Ole Nassau Coconut Rum
1 oz. Ann's Cove 151° rum
1 oz. pineapple juice

½ oz. lemon juice
½ oz. Grenadine
½ oz. Ole Nassau
  Pineapple Rum

Garnish with a slice of pineapple.

DESPERATE VIRGIN
2 ozs. Ole Nassau Coconut Rum
2 ozs. orange juice
1½ ozs. pineapple grapefruit juice

½ oz. Grenadine
1 oz. Appleton 151° Rum

Garnish with lots of cherries.

LULLABY BABY
2 ozs. Ole Nassau Coconut Rum
½ oz. lemon juice
2 ozs. pineapple juice

½ oz. Syrup
1 oz. Matusalem

Garnish with a slice of orange.

PILOT HOUSE HOTEL PINACOLADO
1¼ ozs. Mount Gay Rum
3 ozs. pineapple juice
¾ ozs. Ole Nassau Coconut Rum

2 ozs. evaporated milk
Dash of simple syrup

Shake well and serve in a tall glass with ice.

PINEAPPLE COCKTAIL

1 jigger pineapple rum
½ dry vermouth
2 dashes Creme de Cacao
Juice of one lime

Stir well with ice and strain into a glass.

PINEAPPLE FLIP

2 jiggers pineapple rum
1 egg
1 teaspoon powdered sugar

Shake well with cracked ice and strain into a glass. Sprinkle nutmeg on top.

PINEAPPLE MIST FIZZ

2 ozs. pineapple rum
1 oz. pineapple juice (unsweetened)
½ teaspoon powdered sugar

Shake with ice. Strain into highball glass. Fill **with** carbonated water and stir.

PINE 'N PINE

2 jiggers pineapple rum
1 jigger Kummel
1 jigger orange juice
1 dash pimento dram

Shake well with shaved ice and strain into glasses.

PINEAPPLE SUNSHINE

1½ ozs. pineapple rum
1½ ozs. sweet vermouth

Stir with ice and strain into cocktail glass.

WHISKY BASED DRINKS

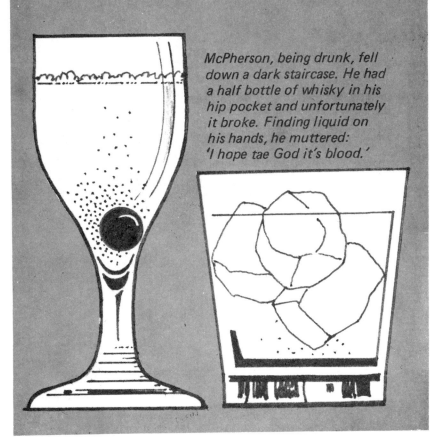

McPherson, being drunk, fell down a dark staircase. He had a half bottle of whisky in his hip pocket and unfortunately it broke. Finding liquid on his hands, he muttered: 'I hope tae God it's blood.'

ARTIST'S SPECIAL

1/3 Whisky   1/6 lemon juice
1/3 sherry   1/6 sugar syrup

Stir well with ice and strain into glass.

BLINKER COCKTAIL

½ oz. Canadian Whisky   ¼ oz. grapefruit juice
¼ oz. Grenadine   Cracked ice

Shake whisky, grapefruit juice and Grenadine with cracked ice.
Serve in chilled cocktail glass.

BOBBY BURNS

½ part Scotch Whisky   1 dash Benedictine
¼ part dry vermouth   Ice cubes
¼ part sweet vermouth   Lemon peel

Stir Scotch, dry and sweet vermouth and Benedictine with ice and
serve in 2½ oz. cocktail glass. Garnish with twist of lemon peel.

CREOLE

½ Whisky   2 dashes Benedictine
½ sweet vermouth   2 dashes Amer Picon

Stir with ice and strain into glass. Serve with twist of lemon peel

DUPPY

Pour 6 jiggers of whisky into a mixing glass and add a few cloves. Let
soak about 1 hour. Add 5 or 6 drops orange bitters and 1 jigger
Curacao. Shake well with ice and strain into glasses. Serves 6.

FLU

2 jiggers Rye Whiskey   1 dollop Jamaica Rum
1 teaspoon ginger brandy   Juice of ¼ lemon
1 teaspoon Rock Candy syrup

Stir well without ice and strain into glass.

HOT DECK

¾ Rye Whiskey   1 dash Jamaica ginger
¼ sweet vermouth

Shake well with ice and strain into glass.

HOT FLASHES

2 ozs. Whisky
1/2 oz. Campari
Lemon peel

1/4 oz. Bianco Vermouth
Ice

Mix whisky, Campari and vermouth with ice in a mixing glass.
Serve with lemon peel in a cocktail glass.

LINSTEAD

1 part Scotch Whisky   1 part sweetened pineapple juice
Shake together with a dash of Pastis and add a twist of lemon peel.

MAMIE TAYLOR

2 ozs. Scotch Whisky
I ce

Ginger ale
Slice of lemon

Serve scotch in 10 oz. glass with ice. Top with ginger ale and slice of lemon

MANHATTAN (DRY)

1 1/2 ozs. Canadian Whisky
3/4 oz. dry vermouth
1 or 2 dashes Angostura Bitters (optional)

Ice
Twist of lemon or olive

Stir whisky, vermouth and bitters with ice and strain into 3 oz. cocktail
glass. Add twist of lemon peel or olive and serve.

MANHATTAN (MEDIUM)

4 parts Rye (Canadian) Whisky   1 part sweet vermouth
1 part dry vermouth

Mix together and serve

MANHATTAN (SWEET)

1 1/2 ozs. Canadian Whisky
3/4 oz. sweet vermouth
1 dash Angostura Bitters (optional).

Ice
Maraschino Cherry

Stir whisky, vermouth and bitters with ice and strain into 3 oz. cocktail
glass. Garnish with Maraschino Cherry.

MODERN No. 2

2 jiggers Scotch Whisky
1 dash lemon juice
1 dash Pernod

2 dashes Jamaica Rum
1 dash orange bitters

Stir well with ice, strain into glass and serve with a cherry.

MORNING GLORY

1½ ozs. Scotch Whisky
White of egg
Soda water

1 teaspoon castor sugar
Ice

Shake Scotch, egg white and castor sugar, then strain into a highball glass with ice. Top with soda water and serve.

OLD-FASHIONED

Pour into a tumbler 1—2 teaspoonsful sugar syrup and add 1—3 dashes of Angostura. Stir to blend them. Add a little rye or Bourbon and stir again. Add 2 large ice cubes. Stir. Fill with more whisky nearly to the top. Stir. Add a zest of lemon to the glass. Decorate with a cherry and serve with a spoon to stir further.

ROB ROY

½ part Scotch Whisky
½ part sweet vermouth

1 dash Angostura Bitters
1 Maraschino Cherry

Stir scotch vermouth and bitters in mixing glass with ice. Pour into 3 oz. cocktail glass, add cherry and serve.

RUSTY NAIL

Pour 2 parts Scotch Whisky and 1 part Drambuie over ice in old-fashioned glass. Serve with a twist of lemon peel.

WHISKY COCKTAIL

4 parts Scotch Whisky
1 part Orange Curacao

2 dashes Angostura Bitters

Mix together, add a cherry and serve.

WHISKY MILK PUNCH

2 ozs. Scotch Whisky
½ pint milk

1½ teaspoons sugar
Nutmeg

Shake Scotch, milk and sugar with ice and strain into a highball glass. Sprinkle nutmeg on top and serve.

WHISKY-ON-THE-ROCKS

Serve 2 ozs. Scotch Whisky in old-fashioned glass with ice cubes.

WHIZZ BANG

2 parts Scotch Whisky
1 part dry vermouth
2 dashes Orange Bitters

2 dashes Pastis
2 dashes Grenadine

Mix together and serve.

68

BRANDY BASED DRINKS

Not an ascent from body to spirit, but the descent of spirit into body.
— N.O. Brown.

BARBADOS HOP

1 oz. brandy   ½ oz. rum
½ straight Bourbon Whisky   Juice 1 lemon
1 tablespoon powdered sugar

Shake all ingredients with ice and strain into collins glass with cubed ice. Fill with carbonated water and stir.

BETWEEN-THE-SHEETS

1/3 brandy
1/3 Cointreau   1/3 light rum

Shake well with ice and strain into glass.

BOSOM CARESSER

2/3 brandy   Yolk of 1 egg
1/3 orange Curacao   1 teaspoon Grenadine

Shake together brandy, Curacao, egg yolk and Grenadine.
Pour into 3 oz cocktail glass and serve.

BRANDY ALEXANDER

1/3 brandy   1/3 Creme de Cacao
1/3 fresh cream   Nutmeg

Shake brandy, Creme de Cacao and fresh cream with ice.

Strain into 6 oz. champagne glass.

Serve with nutmeg sprinkled on top.

CARNIVAL

1 part brandy   1 part Lillet
1 part apricot brandy   1 dash Kirsch
1 dash orange juice

Shake together and serve.

CHERRY BLOSSOM

2 parts brandy   1 dash orange Curacao
3 parts cherry brandy   1 dash lemon juice
1 dash Grenadine

Shake together and serve.

CITY SLICKER

2/3 brandy
1 dash Pernod   1/3 Curacao

Shake well with ice and strain into glass.

COFFEE COCKTAIL

1 1/3 ozs. brandy
1 1/3 ozs. green Creme de Menthe

Shake brandy and Creme de Menthe
Strain into 3 oz. cocktail glass and serve.

COFFEE COCONUT

1 oz. brandy
1 coconut
3 cubes ice

1 oz. Sangster's Coffee
Liqueur
Nutmeg

Take off top of coconut and remove milk.
Place half the milk and ice cubes into cocktail shaker.
Add brandy and Tia Maria, then shake and strain back into the coconut. Dust with nutmeg and serve with spoon and drinking straws.

CUBAN

2 parts brandy
1 part apricot brandy

1 part fresh lime juice

Shake together and serve.

DEVIL COCKTAIL

1 1/3 ozs. brandy
1 1/3 Creme de Menthe

Shake brandy and Creme de Menthe and strain into 3 oz. cocktail glass and serve.

EAST INDIA

¾ brandy
1/8 pineapple juice

1/8 Curacao
1 dash Angostura Bitters

Stir well with ice and strain into glass.

FRENCH CONNECTION

1½ ozs. dry gin
1 teaspoon powdered sugar
Juice of ½ lemon

3 ozs. champagne
Cracked ice
Twist of lemon

Combine gin, sugar, lemon juice and shake with ice.
Strain into 12" highball glass containing ice.
Fill with champagne and add twist of lemon to serve.

GRENADIER

2/3 brandy
1/3 ginger brandy

1 dash Jamaica ginger
1 teaspoon powdered sugar

Stir well with ice and strain into glass.

HORSE'S NECK

1½ ozs. brandy
2 dashes Angostura Bitters
4 cubes ice

1 lemon
Dry ginger ale

Peel the skin of lemon in one piece. Place one end of the peel over the edge of a 10 oz. highball glass (giving the effect of a horse's neck. Fill glass with ice cubes. Add brandy and Angostura Bitters, top dry ginger ale and serve.

JAMAICA GRANITO

1½ ozs. Jamaica Brandy
1 small scoop lemon or orange sherbet

1 oz. Curacao

Combine in collins glass and fill balance with carbonated water and stir. Sprinkle nutmeg on top.

PORT-OF-SPAIN PUNCH

Juice 1 dozen lemons

Pour over large block of ice in punch bowl and stir well.
Add enough powdered sugar to sweeten.

Then add:

1½ qt. brandy
1 pt. peach brandy
1 pt. apple rum

1 qt. tonic water
1 pt. strong tea (optional)

Stir well and decorate with fruits in season.

Serve in punch glasses.

PUERTO RICO HOP

1 oz. brandy
½ oz. straight Bourbon Whisky
1 tablespoon powdered sugar

Juice 1 lemon
½ oz. rum

Shake all ingredients with ice and strain into collins glass with cubed ice.
Fill with carbonated water and stir.

72

CAMPARI BASED DRINKS

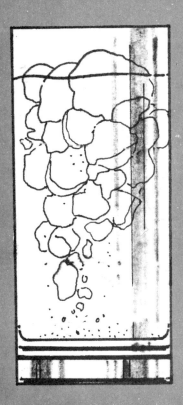

As if you could kill time without injuring eternity.

— Thoreau.

AMERICANO

Pour 1 oz. Campari and 1 oz. Italian vermouth over cracked ice.

Add a twist of lemon peel.

BAHAMIAN DELIGHT
(Mike's Favourite)

Mix equal parts of Campari and grapefruit juice and serve with ice and top off with a cherry.

CAMPARI & SODA

Pour 2 ozs. Campari over ice in a tall glass.

Fill with soda and stir.

CAMPARI & TONIC

Pour 2 ozs. Campari over ice in a tall glass.

Fill with tonic water and serve.

LENA COCKTAIL

(Winner of the International Cocktail Competition held in Tokyo in 1971.)

5/10 Bourbon	1/10 Campari
2/10 Martini Rossi Vermouth	1/10 Galliano
1/10 dry vermouth	1 Maraschino cherry

Stir bourbon, M.R. vermouth and dry vermouth, Campari and Galliano in mixing glass. Serve with cherry.

NEGRONI

1 oz. Campari
1 oz. Italian sweet vermouth
1 oz. gin

Shake ingredients with ice and strain into a cocktail glass.

Stir and serve.

SHERRY BASED DRINKS

A minister came upon a member of his flock staggering home and gave him a helping hand. He was pressed to enter the house but demurred. 'Oh, come on, Man!' he was urged. 'Let the wife see who I I have been out with tonight!'

BAMBOO COCKTAIL

1½ ozs. dry sherry   1 dash orange bitters
¾ oz. dry vermouth
Stir with ice and strain into a cocktail glass, adding a twist of lemon peel.

BRAZIL

1 part dry sherry   1 dash Angostura Bitters
1 part dry vermouth   1 dash Pastis
Mix together and add a twist of lemon peel.

CORONATION

1 part sherry   1 dash Maraschino
1 part dry vermouth   2 dashes orange bitters
Mix together with ice and strain into cocktail glass.

CUPID

2 jiggers Sherry   1 teaspoon powdered sugar
1 egg   1 pinch Cayenne pepper
Shake well with ice and strain into glass.

GREENBRIAR

2 parts dry sherry
1 part dry vermouth
Mix together with ice, a dash of peach bitters and add a sprig of mint.

MARIA

2 ozs. sweet sherry   3 cubes ice
1 oz. Beefeater Gin   1 Maraschino Cherry

Stir sherry and gin with ice cubes in mixing glass, then strain into cocktail glass. Serve with cherry for decoration.

SHERYL TWIST

2 parts dry sherry   1 part Scotch Whisky
2 parts orange juice   2 dashes Cointreau
Shake together and serve with ice.

BEER
BASED
DRINKS

The local publican once acted
as an usher at a funeral and
asked the mourners to pass
around the bier.

Red Stripe Beer...

The Jamaican beer of world renown first brewed in 1928, Red Stripe Beer is made from malt corn hops and water. Like many cities who have built their reputation on beer, i.e. Copenhagen in Denmark, Amsterdam in Holland, Burton-on-Trent in England, Munich in West Germany, Milwaukee in the U.S.A., Kingston is on its way to build its name on Red Stripe; a beer of international reputation.

BEER BUSTER

Ice cold beer
1½ ozs. 100 proof vodka

2 dashes Tabasco Sauce

Put vodka in a highball glass and fill up with beer. Add Tabasco Sauce and stir lightly.

BEER CUP

1 bottle lager beer
1½ ozs. gin
Juice of ½ lemon

1 bottle ginger beer
Soda water
Slice of cucumber

Mix together beer, gin, ginger beer and lemon juice and a splash of soda water.

Garnish with a cucumber slice and a sprig of mint.

Add ice and stir slightly.

BLUE MOUNTAIN PUNCH

3 pts. warmed beer
1 teaspoon Jamaican powdered ginger
1 teaspoon grated nutmeg

¼ pt. rum
3 eggs

2 tablespoons molasses

Blend ginger and nutmeg with 2½ pts. beer and beat.

Beat eggs with remaining ½ pt. beer and molasses.

Mix the two together, a little at a time, beating all the time, add the rum at the same time beat and serve.

BOILERMAKER

1 large jigger of Scotch Whisky served straight with a glass of beer as a chaser.

CARROT PUNCH

1 pt. beer
1½ pts. water

6 medium carrots (grated)
1 cup condensed milk

Make carrot juice, using water.

Sweeten with condensed milk. Add beer and a dash of bitters. Serve chilled over ice cubes.

CHOCOLATE BEER MALT

3 pts. beer
1 tin condensed milk

6 scoops ice cream
(chocolate)

Mix the beer and milk together. Pour in blender and mix at medium speed.

Add ice cream and crushed ice. Mix at high speed until mixture thickens.

Serve immediately.

KOLA BEER

1 pt. lager beer
½ pt. Cola

6 ice cubes

Pour beer in a beer mug and top up with cola.
Add ice cubes and stir lightly.

POLICEMAN GLOW

1 pt. beer
3 jiggers rum

1 tin pineapple juice
Pinch of nutmeg or
cinnamon

Mix all ingredients, shake well.

Pour crushed ice in old-fashioned glasses.

Garnish with orange or pineapple slice.

RED EYE

½ cold beer

½ tomato juice

Mix beer with tomato juice and serve in 10 oz. glass.
A good pick-me-up drink for those 'mornings after.'

RED STRIPE COOLER

8 ozs. beer
8 ozs. tomato juice

½ teaspoon lime juice

Mix ingredients together. Serve on ice in a tall glass.

SHANDY

½ beer
½ lemonade
Mix beer with ice-cold lemonade

SHANDY GAFF

5 ozs. beer
5 ozs. ginger ale
Pour into collins glass and stir.

VIRGIN ISLANDS CREME PUNCH

2 bottles beer
6 eggs
2½ tins condensed milk
1½ tins evaporated milk
Juice of lime

½ pint white rum
3 teaspoons Angostura
bitters
½ teaspoon nutmeg
1 teaspoon vanilla

Whip eggs with lime. Add rum, milk and bitters and blend well. Add beer and serve over crushed ice.

Garnish with a twist of lime peel or lime slices.

WOODPECKER

¾ cup beer
2 medium mangoes
3 slices pineapple
1¼ cups orange juice

3 tablespoons sugar
1 tablespoon lime juice
3 cups water

Blend together mango, pineapple slices, orange juice and sugar. Pour into large jug, add water and beer.

Serve in long, slender glasses over crushed ice with a twist of lime peel.

OTHER ASSORTED DRINKS

'Sarah,'
said Abe,
'call a vet.
I am sick.'
'I'll call a doctor,'
'I don't vant de
doctor I vant a vet.
'Vy a vet?'
'I vork like a horse,
live like a dog, and
sleep with a Cow.'

ACAPULCO

1 jigger Tequila
1 jigger Jamaica rum

2 jiggers pineapple juice
½ jigger grapefruit juice

Shake well with ice cubes.

ARTILLERY PUNCH

1 quart strong black tea
1 quart rye whiskey
1 bottle red wine
1 pint Jamaica rum
½ pint dry gin

½ pint brandy
1 jigger Benedictine
1 pint orange juice
½ pint lemon juice

Combine all ingredients in a large punch bowl with a block of ice. Add sugar syrup if punch is too dry. Decorate with twists of lemon peel. Makes 25 to 30 cups.

BAMBOO

½ sherry

½ sweet vermouth

1 dash Angostura Bitters
Stir well with ice and strain into glass.

BERMUDA BOUQUET

1½ ozs. dry gin
1 oz. apricot brandy
1 teaspoon Grenadine
1 teaspoon powdered sugar

½ teaspoon Triple Sec
Juice ½ lemon
Juice ¼ orange

Shake with ice and strain into highball glass with ice cubes.

BERMUDA HIGHBALL

¾ oz. brandy
¾ oz. dry vermouth

¾ oz. dry gin

Pour into highball glass over ice cubes. Fill with ginger ale or carbonated water.

Add a twist of lemon peel, if desired, and stir.

BISHOP'S COOLER

2 jiggers Burgundy
½ jigger Appleton Dark Rum
1/3 jigger orange juice

1/3 jigger lemon juice
1 teaspoon sugar
2 dashes Angostura Bitters

Place in large highball glass, fill with shaved ice, stir well and serve.

BLACK POWER

2 ozs. Marsala (dessert wine)　　　3 cubes ice
Coca-Cola　　　　　　　　　　　　Slice lemon

Top Marsala with Coca-Cola over ice cubes in old-fashioned glass.
Add slice of lemon and serve.

BLOODY BULL

1 jigger Tequila　　　　　　　　　Dash of Worcestershire
½ jigger lemon juice　　　　　　　and Tabasco

Mix over ice in large glass. Fill with Bouillon and tomato juice, half
and half.

CAYMAN GIRL

¾ oz. sweet cream　　　　　　　　¾ oz. Appleton Rum
¾ oz. Curacao

Shake with ice and pour into cocktail glass.

CHARLES COCKTAIL

1½ ozs. sweet vermouth　　　　　　1 dash bitters
1½ ozs. brandy

Shake with ice and strain into old-fashioned glass over ice cubes.

DOCTOR FUNK

12/3 Jiggers Martinique Rum　　　　1/8 jigger Grenadine
1/8 jigger Pernod　　　　　　　　¼ teaspoon sugar
1/3 jigger lemon juice　　　　　　　1 lime

Cut lime in half and squeeze into shaker, dropping in the rinds also.
Add all other ingredients and shake with crushed ice.
Pour into 12-ounce glass and if necessary, fill with soda water.
Decorate with fruit if desired.

DOMINICAN FESTIVAL

½ jigger apricot brandy　　　　　　½ jigger cream
½ jigger creme de cacao　　　　　1 teaspoon Grenadine

Shake well with ice and strain into large cocktail glass.

FESTIVAL PUNCH

1 quart Jamaica rum
1 quart sweet apple cider
2 or 3 sticks cinnamon, broken

2 teaspoons ground allspice
(pimento)
1 or 2 tablespoons butter

Heat ingredients in a heavy saucepan until almost boiling.
Serve hot in mugs. Serves about 10.

FISH HOUSE PUNCH

A celebrated Philadelphia Club recipe of 1732.

12 ozs. sugar
3 pints water
1½ pints lemon juice

2 bottles rum
1 bottle grape brandy
4½ ozs. peach brandy

Dissolve the sugar in a little water in the punchbowl.

Add the lemon and the rest of the water, stirring well.

Add the rum, grape brandy and peach brandy.

Stir and allow to stand for several hours.

Before serving put a big block of ice in the bowl. Serve when cold.

GLOGG

Pour the following into a kettle:

2 bottles wine (port, sherry, claret, burgundy or Madeira).
2 ozs. dried orange peel

Insert cheese cloth bag containing:

2 ozs. dried orange peel
20 cardamom seeds

2 ozs. cinnamon sticks
25 cloves

Boil slowly for 15 minutes, stirring occasionally.

Add one pound each blanched almonds and seedless raisins and continue to boil for additional 15 minutes.

Remove kettle from stove and place wire grill containing one pound lump sugar over opening.

Pour 1/5 of brandy over sugar making sure to saturate all of it. Then light sugar with match and let it flame.

After sugar has melted, replace kettle cover to extinguish flame. Stir again and remove spice bag.

Serve hot in punch cups with a few almonds and raisins.

GROG

A toddy made with dark rum and lemon juice.

A hot-buttered rum is similar, with a slice of butter instead of lemon juice.

GRASSHOPPER

2/3 jigger green Creme de Menthe   2/3 jigger cream
2/3 jigger white Creme de Cacao

Shake well with ice and serve in champagne glass.

GRIM CHASER

¼ Grand Marnier   ¼ lemon juice
¼ Curacao   ¼ Grenadine

Stir well with ice and strain into glass.

HOT BARBADOS RUM EGG NOG

Mix equal measures of rum and brandy with 1 egg and 1 teaspoonful of sugar in a tall glass.

Fill with hot milk. Stir and add grated nutmeg.

HOT BUTTERED RUM

2 jiggers Jamaica Rum   1 or 2 cloves
1 twist lemon peel   Boiling cider
2 stick cinnamon   Butter

Place rum, lemon peel, clove and cinnamon in a pewter tankard or heavy mug. Fill with boiling cider. Float a pat of butter on top and stir well.

HOT PANTS

1½ ozs. Tequila   1 tablespoon unsweetened
2 ozs. peppermint schnapps   grapefruit juice
1 teaspoon powdered sugar

Shake with ice cubes and pour into old-fashioned glass rimmed with salt.

HUMPTY DUMPTY

2/3 dry vermouth   1/3 Maraschino

Stir well with ice and strain into glass.

LIMEY

1 oz. Appleton Rum   ½ oz. Curacao
1 oz. lime liqueur   2 teaspoons lime juice

Combine ingredients with half a cup of crushed ice in a blender. Blend at low speed and pour into champagne glass. Add a twist of lime peel.

LOLLYPOP GIRL

2 jiggers Cointreau   2 jiggers Kirsch
2 jiggers Chartreuse   1 dash Maraschino

Shake well with ice and strain into glasses. Serve after dinner.

MYRTLE BANK PUNCH

1 jigger Demerara Rum 151 Proof   6 dashes Grenadine
Juice of ½ lime
1 teaspoon sugar

Combine in shaker with a large piece of ice. Shake and pour over cracked ice in a 10-ounce glass. Float Maraschino Liqueur on top.

PANTOMIME

1 jigger dry vermouth   1 dash Grenadine
1 egg white   1 dash Orgeat syrup

Shake well with ice and strain into glass.

PERFECT

1 jigger dry vermouth   1 jigger dry gin
1 jigger sweet vermouth

Stir well with ice and strain into glass. Serve with twist of lemon peel.

PICADOR

2 parts Tequila
1 part Kahlua or Tia Maria or Sangster's Blue Mountain Coffee Liqueur.

Stir well and ice.

Blue Murder

PINEAPPLE CARIBBEAN

1 pineapple
3 cubes ice
1 oz. vodka
1 oz. dark Bacardi
½ oz. apricot brandy

½ oz. cherry brandy
1 dash Angostura Bitters
12 Maraschino cheeries
Lemon slices
1 olive

Slice top off pineapple about 2" from top.

Hollow out the pineapple and cut half the fruit into small squares. Place fruit back in pineapple.

Into cocktail shaker put ice cubes, vodka, Bacardi, apricot brandy, cherry brandy and bitters, and shake.

Pour unstrained over the fruit in the pineapple shell.

Place 4 toothpicks around the edge of the pineapple shell and cover with 3 cherries on each toothpick.

Place 4 toothpicks in lid of pineapple to correspond with position of bottom toothpicks.

Place lid back so that toothpicks go into the cherries.

Decorate with 2 slices (round) of lemon ¼ " thick; one slice of lemon goes on either side of pineapple.

Balance two crossed swizzle sticks on toothpick that goes through the lemon.

Secure the sticks by placing an olive on the exposed part of the toothpick. Serve with spoon and drinking straws.

SANTA CRUZ RUM DAISY

Fill a goblet 1/3 full of shaved ice and add 3 dashes of sugar syrup, 3 dashes Maraschino or Curacao, juice of ½ lemon and fill with rum. Shake well and strain into glass.

SONS OF NEGUS

Heat 1 bottle of Sherry or Port and place in a pitcher. Rub a little lemon rind on 6 cubes of sugar and add to the mixture. Also add 2—3 large twists of rind and the juice of 1 lemon. Add 10 drops of vanilla and 2 cups of boiling water. Sweeten to taste if necessary and strain into glasses. Add a grating of nutmeg and serve. Makes 8 cups.

SPANISH TOWN COCKTAIL

2 ozs. Appleton Rum
1 teaspoon Triple Sec

Stir with ice and strain into cocktail glass.

SPECIAL JAMAICAN RUM PUNCH (HOT)

1 bottle rum
2 lemons
4 ozs. sugar
Up to 3½ pints boiling water.

1 bottle brandy
½ bottle sherry
1 teaspoonful ginger
Grated nutmeg

Grate the rind of the lemons into a small earthenware bowl and add sugar. Macerate sugar and lemon gratings add the juice of lemons and the ginger.

Mix well and place in another large earthenware bowl previously heated. Then add, in the following order: rum, brandy, sherry and boiling water.

Mix well, sweeten further if desired   and stand near heat for 20 minutes before serving in glasses of mugs, with a grating of nutmeg on top.

WEST INDIAN PUNCH

2 qts. rum
1/5 creme de banana
1 qt. pineapple juice
1 qt. orange juice
1 qt. lemon juice

¾ cup powdered sugar
1 teaspoon grated nutmeg
1 teaspoon cinnamon
½ teaspoon grated cloves

Dissolve sugar and spices in 6 oz. carbonated water. Pour into large punch-bowl over block of ice, and add other ingredients. Stir and decorate with sliced bananas.

ZOMBIE

2 ozs. light rum
1 oz. Jamaican rum
½ oz. apricot brandy
½ teaspoon powdered sugar
½ oz. lemon juice
Mint, pineapple, cherry for
  decoration
½ oz. 150° proof Demerara Rum

1 tablespoon (or 1 teaspoon)
Papaya nectar and/or 1
  bar-spoon pineapple juice
  and/or
1 bar-spoon passion fruit
  juice and/or 1 bar-spoon
  plum or apricot juice
Shaved ice and cracked ice

Fill 14 oz. zombie glass with shaved ice. In cocktail shaker put all above ingredients, except Demerara Rum and shake well with cracked ice. Pour unstrained into 14 oz. zombie glass which is ½ full of cracked ice. Decorate with sprig of mint or pineapple spear and cherry. Top with Demarara Rum, being careful to pour so that it floats on surface of drink.

Serve with drinking straws.

NON-ALCOHOLIC DRINKS

He walked in Flavin's Bar and asked for a glass of water. He drank it and walked out. The next day he returned and did the same. 'Here complained the barman, 'You come in here, ask for a glass of water, drink it and then walk... 'What do you want me to do... stagger?'

91

BOO BOO'S SPECIAL

3 ozs. pineapple juice | 1 dash Angostura Bitters
3 ozs. orange juice | 1 dash Grenadine
¼ lemon juice | Pineapple fruit in season
Water | Ice

In cocktail shaker with ice, mix lemon, pineapple and orange juices, Angostura bitters and Grenadine. Shake and serve in tall highball glass. Garnish with pineapple or fruit in season.

HIMBERSHAFT

1 part raspberry syrup to 4 parts soda water.

JUDY'S PUNCH (Approx. 20 drinks)

Any fruit in season or 2 tins fruit salad in punch bowl.

Add cracked ice | 13 ozs. lemon cordial
8 dashes Angostura Bitters | 32 ozs. lemonade
32 ozs. soda water | 2 ozs. Grenadine for colour

Mix ingredients and serve with fruit from bowl.

LEMONADE

Juice of 1 lemon | 1 slice lemon
2 tablespoons sugar | Water
Cracked ice

Fill tall glass with cracked ice and add lemon juice and sugar. Shake and pour unstrained into glass.

Top with water. Slice lemon in drink. Serve with drinking straws.

LIMEADE

Juice 3 limes | 1 Maraschino cherry
3 teaspoons powdered sugar | Cracked ice
Water

Fill tall glass with cracked ice and add lime juice and sugar.

Top with water and mix thoroughly.

Garnish with cherry and serve with drinking straws.

MICKEY MOUSE

Ice | Whipped cream
Coca-Cola | 1 scoop ice cream

Pour Coca-Cola in tall glass with ice. Add 1 scoop ice cream. Top with whipped cream. Serve with 2 cherries, drinking straw and spoon.

NASEBERRY NECTAR

6 Naseberries peeled and seeded   Juice of 1 orange
1 cup sugar   1 cup water

Put all ingredients through a blender.

Strain and serve chilled.

RAIL SPLITTER

Juice of ½ lemon
2/3 jigger sugar syrup

Pour into glass with ice and fill up with ginger beer.

SARATOGA NO.2

Juice of ½ lemon   2 dashes Angostura Bitters
½ teaspoon powdered sugar   Ginger ale

Place ingredients in tall glass with ice cubes and fill with ginger ale.

SOURSOP PUNCH

1 ripe Soursop   Condensed milk to taste
4 glasses water   Vanilla to flavour

Peel and crush soursop, removing seeds.

Stir in water and strain. Add milk and flavouring. Serve ice cold.

SUMMER FIZZ (for 8)

12 sprigs mint   1 cup cold water
½ cup lemon juice   3 cups orange juice
1 cup currant jelly   1 bottle ginger ale
1 cup hot water

Crush mint in a bowl and add boiling water and 1 cup currant jelly. When jelly is melted, add cold water. Strain when cold into punch bowl. Add fruit juices and block of ice. Just before serving, pour in ginger ale and decorate with mint.

TEETOTALLERS PUNCH (Approx. 20 drinks)

½ (13 ozs.) bottle kola   26 ozs. dry ginger ale
3 ozs. lemon juice   26 ozs. lemonade
10 dashes Angostura   Lemon slices
  bitters

Mix all ingredients with cracked ice in punch bowl. Add lemon slices and serve.

PICK-ME-UPS

(OR 'THE MORNING AFTER')

Ring down the curtain, the farce is over!

— Francois Rabelais

CORPSE REVIVER

Shake together 1 part brandy, 1 part Fernet Branca and 1 part White Creme de Menthe.

PICK-ME-UP LICK-ME-DOWN COCKTAIL

1 part cognac with 1 part dry vermouth and 1 part Pastis.

PRAIRIE OYSTER NO. 1

1 jigger brandy
1 dash Worcestershire Sauce

1 egg
salt if desired

Carefully break egg into 6 oz. glass. Add Worcestershire Sauce and brandy. Blend lightly with egg white, keeping yolk intact. For the morning after.

94

*A*Caribbean vacation does not last forever and one will have to face those December months when the mood calls for elegant drink recipes to impart the warmth of a Caribbean sunshine. During my frequent battles with the cold climes I have always found these cocktails my life savers . . .

HOT-BUTTERED RUM (12 Servings)

8 lb butter.
10 lb. brown sugar

½ lb. unsalted butter,
  softened to room temperature
  and cut into pieces.

1/3 cup brown sugar

1 teaspoon nutmeg
1 teaspoon ground cinnamon

A tiny pinch of ground cloves.
1 cup honey

For each individual serving add 1 to 1¼ oz. rum, hot water to taste and a large spoonful of the butter.

To prepare the batter, place ingredients in a large bowl, using a wooden spoon or an electric mixer, cream the butter with brown sugar, nutmeg, cinnamon, cloves and honey. Continue to beat the mixture until the mixture is completely blended and fluffy. The batter will keep if refrigerated for several days. When serving pour the rum into 8 oz. porcelain coffee mugs; fill the mugs with very hot water top with a large spoonful of batter and serve.

IRISH COFFEE

In a 6 oz. glass pour:

¾ oz. Irish Whiskey   Hot Coffee
2 cubes sugar

Heavy cream whipped until stiff with sugar to taste. Pour the whiskey into the glass over 2 cubes of sugar, then pour the coffee down the back of metal spoon; set into the glass (to prevent cracking) remove spoon and top with whipped cream.

TERMINOLOGY

Blazers	—	Drinks that are set alight. For a brandy blazer put a lump of sugar, a twist of lemon peel, a twist of orange peel and a lot of brandy into a flame proof mug or tankard. Light the mixture, stir and strain.
Cobblers	—	Ice and sweetened long drinks with a spirit of wine base. Fine ice goes into the tumbler first followed by the ingredients with the base liquor going in last.
Collins	—	A refreshing long drink made with Dutch gin is called a John Collins; with Old Tom it is called a Tom Collins.
Cordials	—	These are sweetened aromatised spirits and are regarded as heart stimulants.
Fizzes	—	Spirit based long drinks with a form of sweetener; in short a sour made to fizz with soda water or other aerated waters.
Frappes	—	Drinks served with broken or crushed up ice (as opposed to cubes, i.e. 'on the rocks'). The ice goes in first into a long or medium glass followed by a liqueur and two straws. Creme de Menthe frappe compliments your supper on a hot summer night.
Highballs	—	A long iced drink consisting of a base liquid combined with carbonated beverages but without citrus juices.
Rickeys	—	A spirit based drink with fresh limes or other fruit if you are unable to get limes. Gin, Sloe Gin and Rum make the best rickeys.
Smashes	—	Mixed iced drinks flavoured with mint.
Sours	—	Spirit based drinks with citrus fruit juice and usually a sweetener. Also called daises crustas and fixes.
Toddies	—	Usually sweetened hot drinks.

96

YOUR LIQUOR REFERENCE

Amaretto	—	Italy's delicious almond flavoured liqueur.
Anisette 44°	—	Sweetened version of Anis, makes a long drink with bitter lemon, ice and a little lime juice.
Aperitif	—	A drink taken to stimulate one's appetite, usually a wine based cocktail.
Apricot Brandy 42°		A highly flavoured liqueur made from apricots.
Beer		The name for five types of fermented malt beverages: Lager Beer, the most popular type of light; Dry Beer; Ale, having a more pronounced flavour and aroma of hops. It is heavier, more bitter than lager beer and stout.
Benedictine 73°		A sweet herb flavoured brandy based liquor. One of the oldest liqueurs in the world and originally made by The Benedictine Monks. Can be mixed with equal parts of brandy and is sometimes referred to as D.O.M.
Bitters		A blend of roots and herbs used for flavouring. Best known brands are Angostura, Ferñet Branca and Peychauds.
Brandy		Distilled from fermented juice of nice grapes and other fruits. The best of the brandies being cognac.
Calvados		A french apple brandy.
Cherry Brandy 42°		A brandy based in the juices of ripe cherries.
Coconut Milk		Made from the juice of coconut.
Cointreau 70°		A sweet colourless liqueur with orange flavour.
Coconut Rum		Based on the juice of the coconut and fine spirits.
Coconut Liqueur		A delightful liqueur made from the juice of the coconut and blended with spirits.
Creme de Banana 42°		A yellow brandy based liqueur flavoured with bananas.
Creme de Cacao 42°		A very sweet dark liqueur made from cacao beans, vanilla and spices.
Creme de Cassis		A liqueur with black currant flavour.

97

Creme de Menthe	A peppermint flavoured liqueur in green, white or red.
Dubonnet	A dark red French aperitif wine with red wine base and a slight quinine taste.
Galliano 70°	A gold flavoured liqueur with liquorice and anisette flavour.
Gin	Alcohol made from any source of sugar. Tasteless until re-distilled with juniper berries, coriander seeds, angelica roots, calemus, cardamom seeds and orris powder to name the principal flavouring ingredients.
Grand Marnier	French brandy liqueur with orange flavour; brown in colour.
Grenadine	Red artificial flavouring used for sweeteners.
Green Ginger Wine	Wine made from fruit and Jamaican ginger.
Lillet	A French aperitif with white wine base.
Mango Juice	Juice made from the mango fruit.
Maraschino 45°	A colourless cherry flavoured liqueur from Italy and Yugoslavia.
Orange Bitters 70°	Made from the peel of swilles bitter oranges; much used in flavourings.
Papaya Juice/Syrup	Made from the juice of the papaya fruit.
Peach Brandy 45°	A brandy coloured liqueur with peach flavour.
Pimento Liqueur	A liqueur made from the pimento plant which is only to be found in Jamaica; a sharp biting taste.
Schnapps 66.5°	Scandinavian liqueur made from potatoes and flavoured with caraway seeds.
Triple Sec	White Curacao. A colourless liqueur with a sweet orange flavour.
Tequila 66.5°	A Mexican drink made from Pulque — a beverage from the cactus plant also called century plant, agave, mescal. The Mexican way to drink this brew is 'a lick of salt from the back of the hand and a sip of the tequila.'
Vodka	An alcoholic distillate from a fermented mash of grain; it is odourless and colourless.
Whisky	A spirit obtained from distillation of a fermented mash of grain i.e. barley, maize and rice mainly and aged in wood.

INDEX

Rum & Water, 33
Rum Collins, 34
Rum Daiquiri, 24
Rum Daisy, 34
Rum Dubonnet, 34
Rum Frappe, 34
Rum Rickey, 34
Rum Screwdriver, 24
Rum Sour, 34
Russian, 49
Rusty Nail, 68

St. Lucia Jump-Up, 61
Salty Dog, 49
Sandals' Iced Tea, (Sandals III)
Sandals' Pina Colada, (Sandals III)
Sangster's Delight, 57
Santa Cruz Rum Daisy, 89
Santiago, 35
Saratoga No. 2, 93
Satan's Whiskers, 43
Screwdriver, 49
Sea Urchin, 49
Shandy, 80
Shandy Gaff, 80
Shark's Tooth, 35
Sheryl Twist, 76
Singapore Sling, 43
Sons of Negus, 89
Sorrel Appetizer, 35
Soursop Punch, 93
South Side, 44
Spanish Town, 35
Spanish Town Cocktail, 89
Special Jamaican Rum
    Punch (Hot), 90
Starapple Appetizer, 35
Suffering Bastard, 35
Summer Fizz, 93
Sun Stroke, 49
Surprised, 36

T'N'T, 60
Tango, 44
Teetotallers Punch, 93
The Machete, 50

Tia Alexandra, 60
Trinidad, 36
Trinidad Swizzle, 36
Trinity, 44
Tropical Coffee, 57

Virgin Island Twist, 36
Virgin Island's Cocktail, 44
Virgin Island's
    Crème Punch, 80
Virgin's Kiss, (Sandals III)
Vodka Mist, 50
Vodka-On-The-Rocks, 50
Vodka Sour, 50
Vodkatini, 50
Volcano, 50

West Indian Punch, 90
Whisky Cocktail, 68
Whisky Milk Punch, 68
Whisky-On-The-Rocks, 68
White Cargo, 44
White Elephant, 50
White Rum & Sorrel Liquer, 36
White Swan, 61
White Witch, 44
Whizz Bang, 68
Woodpecker, 80

Yellow Bird (Bahamas), 36
Yellow Daisy, 44
Yellow Fever, 50

Zombie, 90